OCEAN DEPTHS YIELD SECRETS

Ocean Depths Yield Secrets

MARITIME MYSTERIES UNVEILED

Alina Hazel

Spectra Enterprise

Contents

Table of Content

Introduction

In the immense region of the world's seas lie stowed away secrets that have long enamored the human creative mind. The charm of sea mysteries, disguised in the profundities, has driven wayfarers and scientists to unwind the mysterious stories that lie underneath the surface. This excursion into the sea's secrets starts with an investigation of the baffling wrecks that rest in its deep profundities, every one holding the possibility to uncover a piece of history that has for quite some time been darkened by the ocean's hug.

One of the most convincing sea secrets is the story of the Franklin Endeavor, a mission for the tricky Northwest Entry that finished in misfortune. The Cold risks looked by Sir John Franklin and his group in the nineteenth century have become inseparable from sea secret. The verifiable setting of this doomed endeavor, driven by the longing to find a traversable course through the Icy, makes way for a sensational investigation into the difficulties looked by the people who really considered wandering into the frozen unexplored world.

As of late, mechanical headways in marine prehistoric studies have carried new bits of knowledge into the Franklin Undertaking. The disclosure of the destruction of HMS Erebus and HMS Dread has given a substantial connection to the past, offering a brief look into the circumstances and occasions that prompted the end of the pioneers. As submerged investigation methods have advanced, so too has our capacity to open the mysteries concealed in the sea's profundities. The Franklin Campaign remains as a demonstration of the crossing point of verifiable interest and state of the art innovation, a story that keeps on unfurling with each new disclosure from the Icy seabed.

The Bermuda Triangle, a locale encompassed in legend and secret, has for some time been related with unexplained vanishings of boats and airplane. This perplexing three-sided region in the western piece of the North Atlantic Sea has filled hypothesis about powerful powers and extraterrestrial peculiarities. Nonetheless, logical examinations concerning the Bermuda Triangle have looked to disperse the fantasies encompassing this infamous stretch of ocean.

Through cautious investigation of authentic records and episode reports, specialists have distinguished regular clarifications for the majority of the supposed vanishings. The Bermuda Triangle, it appears, isn't a hotbed of paranormal action yet rather a locale inclined to unusual and serious weather patterns. Maverick waves, attractive inconsistencies, and human mistake have all added to the standing of the Bermuda Triangle as a position of secret and risk. By demystifying this once-baffling peculiarity, researchers have reshaped how we might interpret the dangers looked by mariners and pilots exploring the world's seas.

In the profundities off the shore of Egypt lies the lowered city of Heracleion, a once-flourishing port city that strangely evaporated underneath the waters. The revelation of this depressed city has given archeologists a one of a kind chance to investigate the leftovers of an old human progress protected in the sea's hug. Using submerged innovations, scientists have revealed an abundance of curios and designs that offer bits of knowledge into the regular routine, exchange, and social acts of individuals of Heracleion.

The account of Heracleion features the extraordinary force of submerged prehistoric studies in uncovering lowered treasures. Through careful uncovering and examination, specialists have sorted out the historical backdrop of a city that was lost to the profundities of the Mediterranean. The submerged remnants of Heracleion act as a period case, protecting a depiction of a former time and enhancing how we might interpret the interconnectedness of old developments.

The story of the Mary Celeste, a phantom boat viewed as unfastened adrift in 1872, is one of the persevering through sea secrets that has confused students of history and sea fans for more than hundred years. The boat, apparently deserted, was found in secure condition without any indication of battle or treachery. The vanishing of the team has brought about various speculations, going from robbery to the ocean beasts and extraterrestrial experiences.

Logical examinations concerning the Mary Celeste have tried to unwind the conundrum encompassing the vessel. Scientific investigation and authentic exploration have given conceivable clarifications to the group's strange takeoff. Hypotheses of navigational blunders, catastrophic events, or even a neglected endeavor to arrive at a close by island have been advanced. By isolating reality from fiction, scientists have added to a more nuanced comprehension of this notorious phantom boat peculiarity.

The field of submerged paleohistory, devoted to the investigation and removal of lowered social legacy, assumes a urgent part in revealing oceanic secrets. Particular apparatuses and advances are utilized to explore the difficulties of working in the submerged climate. Remote detecting gadgets, submerged drones, and high level imaging methods have become basic in archiving and saving submerged locales.

Contextual analyses of effective oceanic archeological campaigns exhibit the inventive methodologies taken by scientists. These endeavors not just add as far as anyone is concerned of explicit verifiable occasions yet in addition shed light on the more extensive examples of human relocation, exchange, and social trade. The cooperative energy of mechanical development and verifiable request in submerged paleontology opens new wildernesses in the investigation of our oceanic past.

The protection of submerged social legacy is a basic thought for scientists and policymakers the same. The natural and moral difficulties related with sea paleontology request cautious stewardship of these lowered locales.

The fragile harmony among investigation and conservation requires a smart way to deal with guarantee that people in the future can keep on opening the mysteries concealed in the sea profundities.

Proceeding with our investigation into the profundities of oceanic secrets, the riddle of the Bermuda Triangle fills in as a demonstration of the force of logical request in scattering longstanding legends. Long covered in hypothesis and emotionalism, the Bermuda Triangle, otherwise called "Satan's Triangle," envelops a district limited by focuses in Miami, Bermuda, and Puerto Rico. Throughout the long term, it has been related with the baffling vanishing of boats and airplane, leading to a plenty of speculations going from extraterrestrial obstruction to submerged city ruins.

Be that as it may, as scientists have dug into the verifiable records and directed thorough examinations, a more nuanced comprehension of the Bermuda Triangle has arisen. The alleged paranormal events inside this three-sided territory have been to a great extent credited to regular peculiarities and human mistakes. Maverick waves, attractive abnormalities, and abrupt changes in weather conditions are among the experimentally upheld clarifications for some episodes.

In one remarkable case, Flight 19, a unit of five U.S. Naval force aircraft, vanished over the Bermuda Triangle in 1945. Instead of conjuring otherworldly causes, examiners have highlighted navigational blunders and fuel fatigue as likely clarifications for the group's vanishing. Comparable investigations have been applied to different occurrences, uncovering an example of conceivable, non-strange clarifications.

The logical way to deal with unwinding the secrets of the Bermuda Triangle highlights the significance of decisive reasoning and proof based request. By applying standards of meteorology, oceanography, and flying science, scientists have destroyed the air of persona encompassing this locale, changing it from a shelter of mysterious peculiarities to a zone where realized regular powers can merge in eccentric ways.

Directing our concentration toward the lowered city of Heracleion, off the bank of Egypt, we enter a domain where old civilizations lie buried underneath the sea's surface. Heracleion, otherwise called Thonis, was a clamoring port city that flourished at the mouth of the Nile Delta. Be that as it may, close to quite a while back, it capitulated to catastrophic events, including quakes and rising ocean levels, at last evaporating underneath the waters.

The rediscovery of Heracleion in 2000 denoted a turning point in submerged prehistoric studies. Using cutting edge innovations, for example, sonar planning and submerged unearthing devices, specialists revealed a city frozen in time. Lowered sculptures, sanctuaries, and leftovers of a once-energetic city have given significant experiences into the social and financial trades of the old world.

The conservation of curios in the submerged climate is extraordinary, offering a special chance to concentrate on old materials that would somehow have disintegrated or rotted ashore. Through the careful work of submerged archeologists, the lowered city of Heracleion has turned into a period container, revealing insight into the interconnectivity of old civic establishments and the effect of normal powers on human settlements.

The Mary Celeste, a phantom boat found unfastened in the Atlantic Sea in 1872, epitomizes a sea secret that has powered minds for ages. The boat was tracked down in secure condition, with its freight flawless, yet the team was mysteriously absent. Hypotheses about theft, uprising, and, surprisingly, extraterrestrial experiences proliferated, making a persevering through conundrum that continued for more than a long time.

Logical examinations concerning the Mary Celeste have tried to demystify the conditions encompassing the team's vanishing. Criminological examination of the boat's logs and proof of a hurriedly deserted dinner have driven specialists to propose speculations, for example, navigational blunders or a bombed endeavor to arrive at a close by island. The once-slippery phantom boat has turned into a contextual investigation in isolating reality from fiction, exhibiting how a mix of verifiable examination and logical examination can unwind longstanding oceanic riddles.

Submerged paleohistory, with its specific devices and state of the art advancements, assumes a critical part in exposing these oceanic secrets. Remote detecting gadgets, submerged robots, and high-goal imaging methods have upset the field, empowering analysts to investigate and report lowered destinations with exceptional accuracy. Contextual analyses of fruitful submerged archeological undertakings highlight the potential for these instruments to open the insider facts of the sea's profundities.

As we explore the strange waters of disclosure, taking into account the moral and natural ramifications of sea archeology is essential. Protecting submerged social legacy requires a fragile harmony among investigation and preservation. The sensitive environments encompassing these lowered destinations should be shielded, and antiquities painstakingly figured out how to guarantee their respectability for people in the future.

"Sea Profundities Yield Mysteries: Sea Secrets Uncovered" fills in as a gateway to a world underneath the waves, where verifiable stories are written in the submerged urban communities, spooky ships, and secret relics that lie on pause. From the perspective of logical request and mechanical advancement, these oceanic secrets change from mysterious stories into substantial bits of our common mankind's set of experiences. The sea, when a boundary to our comprehension, turns into a wellspring of disclosure, advising us that the insider facts it monitors are not invulnerable yet anticipate the inquisitive personalities and decided wayfarers who try to dive into its profundities.

Chapter 1

The Mysterious Wrecks of the Deep

The Secretive Wrecks of the Profound

Underneath the huge fields of the world's seas lies a secret universe of sea secrets, where the remainders of old boats lay quietly on the sea floor, covered in obscurity and secret. The investigation of these puzzling wrecks, dissipated across the deep profundities, has turned into an intriguing undertaking for students of history, archeologists, and sea life researchers the same. These indented vessels, once powerful and cruising on a superficial level, have become time cases protecting stories of experience, misfortune, and the oceanic history that formed civilizations.

One of the most interesting parts of these submerged time cases is the variety of wrecks that range various periods and societies. From old wooden vessels to present day steel-hulled ships, the sea floor fills in as a cemetery of oceanic history, holding the narratives of pioneers, brokers, and explorers who explored deceptive waters in quest for new skylines. The safeguarding of these disaster areas vulnerable, dull profundities gives a special chance to uncover the mysteries of days of yore and the difficulties looked by the individuals who cruised the oceans.

The revelation of wrecks uncovers verifiable stories as well as presents an enticing riddle for archeologists trying to sort out the occasions prompting the vessel's downfall. Each disaster area recounts an account of human creativity, mechanical progressions, and the unusual powers of nature that planned to send these vessels to the sea floor. The conservation of curios inside these disaster areas, going from navigational instruments to individual possessions, offers a brief look into the regular routines and battles of the people who cruised the high oceans.

Additionally, wrecks frequently act as markers of huge verifiable occasions, giving substantial proof of maritime fights, shipping lanes, and social trades. The investigation of these submerged archeological destinations can possibly revise history books and challenge existing accounts about old developments and their sea exercises. Through cautious assessment of the disaster areas and their items, scientists can sort out a more extensive comprehension of the interconnected world that existed some time before the appearance of current correspondence and transportation.

The remote ocean investigation of wrecks requires refined innovation and specific gear, like remotely worked vehicles (ROVs) and independent submerged vehicles (AUVs), fit for enduring the outrageous tensions and murkiness of the deep profundities. These devices empower researchers to catch high-goal pictures, record antiquities in situ, and lead harmless reviews that regard the sensitive idea of these lowered time containers. The utilization of trend setting innovation works with investigation as well as limits the effect on the delicate environments encompassing these disaster areas.

Perhaps of the main test in concentrating on remote ocean wrecks is the brutal climate where they live. The huge tension, close frosty temperatures, and nonattendance of light make an unfriendly setting that requests strength from the two voyagers and gear. Regardless of these difficulties, the prizes of revealing the secrets concealed inside these disaster areas are unfathomable, offering an interesting viewpoint on the development of oceanic innovation, exchange, and social trade since the beginning of time.

Notwithstanding their verifiable and archeological importance, wrecks assume a significant part in marine nature by making fake reefs that help different biological systems. The rotting structures give a substrate to the connection of marine life forms, making a lively and dynamic submerged environment. Coral reefs, wipes, and different types of fish find shelter and food around these lowered designs, changing what was once a vessel of human creation into a flourishing biological system overflowing with life.

The investigation of wrecks additionally presents moral contemplations, especially in regards to the conservation and security of these submerged legacy locales.

The charm of significant curios has prompted the ravaging of wrecks by treasure trackers, representing a danger to the honesty of these verifiable locales. Endeavors to adjust the craving for revelation with the requirement for mindful preservation have prompted peaceful accords and rules pointed toward protecting submerged social legacy and advancing moral archeological practices.

The investigation of remote ocean wrecks not just fills in as a window into the past yet additionally brings up issues about the eventual fate of submerged paleohistory and the safeguarding of our sea legacy. As progressions in innovation proceed, the potential for new revelations and a more profound comprehension of the sea's mysteries turns out to be progressively encouraging. The secrets concealed inside the deep profundities are huge and differed, with each disaster area offering a special riddle to tackle.

One angle that adds intricacy to the investigation of submerged wrecks is the powerful idea of the sea floor. The development of structural plates, submerged flows, and the consistent moving of dregs can adjust the scene and cover or uncover wrecks over the long run. This steadily changing climate moves specialists to adjust their investigation procedures and return to destinations to catch new bits of knowledge that might arise because of these regular cycles.

The investigation of wrecks additionally gives significant bits of knowledge into the mechanical progressions of various periods. From antiquated wooden vessels to steamships and maritime warships, the development of sea innovation is in plain view on the sea depths. Figuring out the designing, development strategies, and materials utilized in these vessels adds as far as anyone is concerned of history as well as gives a setting to assessing the advancement of human creativity and advancement in shipbuilding.

Moreover, the investigation of remote ocean wrecks has suggestions for the continuous improvement of marine paleohistory as a discipline. The difficulties of working in outrageous conditions and the requirement for interdisciplinary co-operation between archeologists, sea life researchers, and architects push the limits of our aggregate information. As new strategies and innovations arise, the potential for more exact dating of antiquities, conservation procedures, and information investigation increments, improving our capacity to remove significant data from these lowered time cases.

The meaning of wrecks stretches out past the investigation of individual vessels. It envelops the more extensive oceanic scene, including neglected ports, route courses, and exchange organizations. By planning and concentrating on the dissemination of wrecks, analysts can recreate verifiable seascapes and gain experiences into the interconnectedness of various locales and societies.

This all encompassing way to deal with sea paleontology adds to a more thorough comprehension of the job the seas played in forming mankind's set of experiences.

One amazing illustration of the insider facts uncovered by remote ocean wrecks is the investigation of old shipping lanes. The destruction of boats that once cruised along these courses offers unmistakable proof of the merchandise traded between far off civic establishments. From valuable cargoes of flavors and silks to ordinary things like stoneware and devices, the relics recuperated from these disaster areas give a substantial connection to the financial and social trades that happened across the oceans. This knowledge into the old world's exchange elements advances how we might interpret worldwide associations and the progression of wares that aided mold social orders.

The social meaning of wrecks is additionally apparent in the narratives they tell about individuals who cruised these vessels. Individual things like dress, instruments, and even food remainders offer a brief look into the day to day routines of mariners and travelers. These curios refine the past, permitting us to interface on an individual level with people who lived hundreds of years prior. The profound effect of finding a wreck goes past scholastic interest, encouraging a feeling of compassion for the people who confronted the hazards of the ocean in quest for experience, exchange, or investigation.

While the investigation of remote ocean wrecks is irrefutably entrancing, it isn't without its difficulties and moral contemplations. The fragile idea of these submerged locales requires fastidious intending to guarantee that investigation and recuperation endeavors don't upset the respectability of the disaster areas or the encompassing biological systems. Finding some kind of harmony between logical request and protection is fundamental to saving these submerged time containers for people in the future.

Additionally, the security of wrecks from plundering and unlawful rescue tasks is a continuous concern. The charm of important curios, like gold coins, navigational instruments, or valuable freight, has prompted occurrences of double-dealing and annihilation of submerged social legacy. Global coordinated effort and the execution of lawful structures, for example, the UNESCO Show on the Insurance of the Submerged Social Legacy, look to address these difficulties and lay out rules for dependable investigation and exhuming.

The baffling wrecks of the profound are a demonstration of the getting through charm of the seas and the untold stories that lie underneath the surface. The investigation of these lowered time cases enhances how we might interpret history as well as moves us to consider the moral obligations that accompany disentangling the secrets of the past. As innovation progresses and interdisciplinary coordinated effort keeps on flourishing, the privileged insights concealed inside the sea profundities will undoubtedly dazzle the creative mind of people in the future, guaranteeing that the investigation of oceanic secrets stays a dynamic and developing undertaking.

1.1 Introduction to the allure of maritime mysteries and their hidden stories.

Prologue to the Charm of Oceanic Secrets and Their Secret Stories

The vast scope of the world's seas has long spellbound the human creative mind, moving stories of investigation, experience, and the unexplored world. Inside the profundities of these tremendous waterways lie oceanic secrets, lowered stories ready to be found and revealed. The charm of the sea's mysteries has driven wayfarers, researchers, and students of history to set out on ventures into the deep profundities, trying to disentangle the secret stories that lie underneath the surface.

The interest with sea secrets is well established in the rich embroidered artwork of mankind's set of experiences and the urgent job that the seas have played in molding civilizations. The limitlessness of the oceans, both a wellspring of food and a domain of risk, has been the setting for epic journeys, shipping lanes, and maritime endeavors. As boats cruised into unknown waters, they conveyed with them the expectations, dreams, and at times, the misfortunes of those ready. It is these accounts — of wins and hardships, of lost vessels and found treasures — that permeate sea secrets with a persevering through appeal.

One of the most convincing aspects of oceanic secrets lies in the investigation of wrecks, the depressed leftovers of vessels that once cruised gladly on a superficial level. These submerged time containers offer a substantial association with the past, saving the historical backdrop of nautical societies and the difficulties looked by the people who wandered out from the dark ocean. From old wooden boats to current steel-hulled vessels, each disaster area has a story to tell — an account that traverses the ages and addresses the unstoppable soul of investigation.

The charm of oceanic secrets isn't exclusively restricted to the verifiable records exemplified in wrecks. The remote ocean, with its baffling and frequently dream-like scenes, harbors a plenty of privileged insights ready to be uncovered. From bioluminescent life forms enlightening the haziness to submerged volcanoes molding the World's outside layer, the secrets of the sea profundities reach out past the human-driven accounts to envelop the very powers that have molded our planet more than large number of years.

As innovation has progressed, so too has our capacity to investigate and grasp the secrets of the profound. Subs, remotely worked vehicles (ROVs), and independent submerged vehicles (AUVs) have become vital apparatuses for analysts trying to explore the outrageous states of the deep profundities. These mechanical wonders not just empower us to catch amazing pictures of submerged scenes yet additionally work with the recuperation of antiques and the investigation of marine life right at home.

The appeal of oceanic secrets is additionally entwined with the social and archeological meaning of the disclosures made in the remote ocean. Wrecks, with their freight holds and individual curios, give a brief look into the existences of the people who lived in various periods. The investigation of these lowered time containers adds to how we might interpret shipping lanes, maritime fighting, and the social trades that happened across the oceans. Every revelation adds another layer to the story of mankind's set of experiences, testing assumptions and revealing insight into the interconnectedness of assorted developments.

Past the authentic and archeological aspects, sea secrets spellbind our minds through the sheer variety of life frames that possess the sea profundities. From the profundities of the Mariana Channel to the immense submerged fields, biological systems exist in a fragile equilibrium, adjusted to get by under outrageous circumstances. Abnormal and powerful animals, some of which have never come around, meander the deep profundities, testing how we might interpret life's limits and the potential for extraterrestrial natural surroundings.

The appeal of oceanic secrets stretches out to the geologic wonders concealed underneath the waves. Submerged volcanoes, aqueous vents, and remote ocean channels are spectacular in their scale as well as basic to the World's unique cycles. Concentrating on these highlights gives experiences into plate tectonics, the arrangement of mineral stores, and the job of the seas in managing the planet's environment. The investigation of these geographical marvels adds a logical aspect to the charm, as specialists uncover the insider facts of the World's inward functions.

Moreover, the actual seas, with their tremendous flows and perplexing environments, hold the way to figuring out the more extensive elements of our planet. The investigation of sea secrets adds as far as anyone is concerned of oceanography, environment science, and natural supportability. By concentrating on sea flows, temperatures, and synthetic sytheses in the deep profundities, researchers gain important bits of knowledge into the mind boggling exchange between the seas and the air, with suggestions for environment demonstrating and the alleviation of natural difficulties.

The charm of sea secrets rises above the limits of existence, bringing us into a domain where the past, present, and future unite. It entices travelers and analysts to dig into the obscure, unwinding the secret stories that have molded the course of mankind's set of experiences and keep on forming how we might interpret the world. As we explore the sea profundities, we are stood up to with the acknowledgment that the secrets covered underneath the waves are all around as different and complicated as the actual seas.

One of the getting through allures of oceanic secrets lies in the profound reverberation of wrecks — the quiet observers to the victories and misfortunes of nautical civilizations. The sea floor, embellished with the skeletal remaining parts of vessels from various periods, fills in as a piercing sign of the dangers and vulnerabilities that went with oceanic investigation.

The lumbering wrecks, embellished with corals and occupied by marine life, bring out a feeling of immortality and weakness, underscoring the transient idea of human undertakings despite the immense and strong sea.

The investigation of wrecks, frequently covered in dimness and stowed away from the natural eye for a really long time, addresses a type of submerged time travel. As archeologists carefully report and study these lowered time containers, they uncover relics that give unmistakable associations with individuals who once cruised these vessels. From navigational instruments and individual effects to the freight that filled the holds, every curio recounts a story — an account of endurance, exchange, and the persistent quest for revelation. In sorting out these sections of the past, scientists weave a story that stretches out a long ways past the limits of verifiable records.

In addition, the charm of sea secrets reaches out past the actual remainders of boats to envelop the immaterial accounts of mental fortitude, flexibility, and human resourcefulness. The investigation of wrecks frequently uncovers the exceptional endeavors made by mariners to explore deceptive waters and conquer unexpected difficulties. The stories that rise up out of these submerged investigations commend the human soul — the very soul that impelled mariners into the obscure and propelled them to confront the vulnerabilities of the vast ocean.

The remote ocean, with its deep profundities and strange regions, has turned into a figurative boondocks that fills our aggregate creative mind. It addresses a last wilderness on Earth that matches the limitlessness of space. The investigation of the sea profundities is likened to interstellar excursions, with scientists as cutting edge pioneers furnished with mechanical progressions that empower them to cross the profound and reveal its privileged insights. The charm lies not just in that frame of mind of what is known yet additionally in the expectation of the obscure, helping us that the secrets to remember the profound are a consistently developing investigation of the strange.

Past the human stories and authentic records, the charm of sea secrets is complicatedly attached to the biodiversity that flourishes in the sea profundities. As pioneers dive into the pit, they experience biological systems that oppose regular comprehension, where life adjusts to outrageous tensions, murkiness, and scant assets. The bioluminescent creatures that enlighten the remote ocean make a strange and entrancing scene, testing our biases about the restrictions of life on The planet. The investigation of these submerged biological systems extends our insight into sea life science as well as brings up significant issues about the potential for life in extraterrestrial conditions.

Geographical miracles concealed underneath the waves add one more layer of interest to oceanic secrets. Submerged volcanoes, with their blazing emissions and formation of new landforms, give experiences into the World's powerful cycles.

Aqueous vents, encompassed by extraordinary biological systems, offer a brief look into the transaction among geography and science in the most outrageous conditions. Remote ocean channels, with their amazing profundities, uncover the significant geological highlights that shape the sea floor. Each geographical wonder adds to the complicated account of our planet's development, offering signs about its over a significant time span.

In the mission to comprehend sea secrets, the seas arise as unique and interconnected frameworks that assume a central part in managing the World's environment. The investigation of sea flows, temperature varieties, and compound structures in the deep profundities adds to our understanding of environment elements on a worldwide scale. The sea, with its ability to retain and rearrange heat, impacts weather conditions, and assumes a urgent part in forming the climate we occupy. As we disentangle the secrets of the profound, we gain important bits of knowledge into the fragile equilibrium that supports life on The planet.

The charm of sea secrets, subsequently, lies not just in that frame of mind of individual wrecks or the revelation of remarkable marine species yet in addition in the more extensive comprehension of our planet's interconnected frameworks. It welcomes us to ponder the unpredictable trap of connections between geographical cycles, sea flows, and the different life shapes that occupy the remote ocean. The secrets concealed inside the sea profundities become a focal point through which we view the Earth as a dynamic and consistently evolving element, cultivating a significant appreciation for the intricacies that characterize our planet.

The charm of oceanic secrets is a diverse excursion into the obscure — an excursion that incorporates history, science, and the marvels of the regular world. From the piercing accounts of wrecks and the immaterial soul of investigation to the secrets of submerged biological systems and geographical wonders, the charm brings us into a domain of perpetual interest. As innovation proceeds to progress and our comprehension of the sea extends, the charm of sea secrets will endure, coaxing us to investigate, find, and divulge the secret stories that lie underneath the outer layer of the world's seas.

1.2 Overview of famous shipwrecks and lost vessels that have captivated explorers and researchers.

Popular Wrecks and Lost Vessels

The records of sea history are interspersed by the stories of lost vessels and wrecks that have caught the aggregate creative mind of adventurers, antiquarians, and specialists. These lowered relics, quiet observers to the back and forth movement of human civilization, recount accounts of win and misfortune, of investigation and trade, and of the persevering powers of nature that have entrusted these once-superb vessels to the profundities. As we set out on an investigation of popular wrecks, we navigate the oceans and the ages, experiencing stories that range from old times to the cutting edge period.

Quite possibly of the most notorious wreck that has enthralled travelers and fortune trackers the same is the RMS Titanic. The doomed first trip of this extravagant sea liner in 1912 finished in misfortune when it struck an icy mass and sank in the North Atlantic Sea. The misfortune asserted north of 1,500 lives and made a permanent imprint on sea history. Found by oceanographer Robert Ballard in 1985, the Titanic lies more than 12,000 feet beneath the surface, its leftovers dispersed across the seabed. The boat's relics, including the excellent flight of stairs, the boat's bow, and individual effects, have been recuperated, giving an unpleasant look into the plushness and the human stories that met a watery grave.

Hundreds of years before the Titanic, the Mary Rose, a Tudor warship, met a comparative destiny off the shore of Britain in 1545. The pride of Henry VIII's armada, the Mary Rose sank during a commitment with the French naval force. Rediscovered in the mud of the Solent in 1971, the rescue activity turned into a spearheading accomplishment in submerged prehistoric studies. The very much safeguarded leftovers of the Mary Rose, including cannons, weaponry, and regular things, offer a special window into the maritime fighting of the sixteenth hundred years and the existences of the mariners who served ready.

Moving further back in time, the old wrecks of Uluburun and the Antikythera Wreck give important bits of knowledge into the nautical societies of days of yore. The Uluburun transport, tracing all the way back to around 1300 BCE, was a

Bronze Age vessel that sank off the shoreline of current Turkey. Found in 1982, the disaster area yielded a mother lode of curios, including valuable metals, earthenware production, and exchange merchandise, revealing insight into the broad sea exchange organizations of the time. The Antikythera Wreck, found in 1901 off the shore of the Greek island of Antikythera, uncovered an old mechanical gadget known as the Antikythera System. Dated to the second century BCE, this refined gadget is viewed as perhaps of the earliest simple PC, utilized for anticipating galactic positions and shrouds.

In the domain of investigation, the disastrous Franklin Campaign of the nineteenth century remains as an unfortunate story of Icy investigation turned out badly. Driven by Sir John Franklin, the two boats, HMS Erebus and HMS Dread, set out in 1845 to find the Northwest Entry. In any case, the two vessels became caught in the ice, prompting the death of the whole endeavor. The secret of the Franklin Campaign spellbound wayfarers and scientists for north of 100 years until the disaster areas of the two boats were at long last situated in 2014 and 2016. The revelation gave essential bits of knowledge into the circumstances looked by the team, including openness to lead harming from ineffectively saved canned products.

The spooky outline of the USS Arizona lowered in the waters of Pearl Harbor fills in as a powerful sign of the occasions that push the US into The Second Great War. The USS Arizona, a warship of the U.S. Pacific Armada, was sunk during the unexpected assault by Japanese powers on December 7, 1941. The destruction, presently part of the USS Arizona Commemoration, is both a conflict grave and a dedication to the lives lost right then and there.

The submerged war vessel stays an image of strength and penance, securing the verifiable meaning of Pearl Harbor in the aggregate memory.

In the misleading waters of the Bermuda Triangle, the vanishing of Flight 19, a group of five U.S. Naval force aircraft, in 1945 remaining parts a getting through secret. The airplane, on a standard preparation mission, evaporated suddenly, igniting hypotheses of paranormal peculiarities and extraterrestrial contribution. The Bermuda Triangle, an approximately characterized locale in the North Atlantic, has been related with various vanishings, adding a demeanor of persona to the oceanic legend encompassing this region.

The quest for the remaining parts of the Perseverance, the disastrous boat of Sir Ernest Shackleton's Antarctic undertaking, has been a new focal point of oceanic investigation. The Perseverance was caught and squashed by ice in 1915, constraining Shackleton and his group to leave transport and get through a remarkable excursion to endurance. In 2022, an endeavor drove by the Falklands Oceanic Legacy Trust found the astoundingly all around saved wreck of the Perseverance, lying in north of 3,000 meters of water off the shore of Antarctica. The disclosure carries another section to the tradition of Shackleton's amazing story of authority, strength, and endurance even with affliction.

Every one of these well known wrecks and lost vessels addresses a section in the continuous investigation of the world's seas. The appeal of these oceanic secrets lies in their verifiable importance as well as in the inquiries they present and the tales they keep on telling. The investigation of these lowered time containers adds to how we might interpret maritime engineering, shipping lanes, mechanical headways, and the human stories that stay implanted in the destruction on the sea floor. As innovation advances and investigation methods develop, the secrets of the profound keep on calling, welcoming us to reveal the secret accounts that lie underneath the outer layer of the world's oceans.

Wandering into the waters encompassing the far off Easter Island, the secrets of the USS Indianapolis add one more layer of interest to sea history. Soaking in the last long stretches of The Second Great War in the wake of conveying parts for the nuclear bomb that would later be dropped on Hiroshima, the USS Indianapolis confronted a more dismal destiny — the boat was destroyed by a Japanese submarine, and the survivors persevered through long stretches of openness, drying out, and shark assaults before salvage. The area of the USS Indianapolis stayed obscure for north of seventy years until it was found by donor Paul Allen's examination vessel in 2017. The revelation not just carried conclusion to the groups of the lost mariners yet in addition shed light on the nerve racking experience looked by the team in the vast sea.

In the domain of privateer legend, the amazing wreck of the Whydah Gally keeps on dazzling history specialists and fortune trackers the same. Directed by the famous privateer Samuel "Dark Sam" Bellamy, the Whydah was a slave transport switched privateer vessel that met its end off the shore of Cape Cod in 1717 during a savage tempest.

Found by submerged adventurer Barry Clifford in 1984, the Whydah Gally yielded an exceptional stash of privateer treasure, including gold coins, adornments, and weaponry. The relics not just given a brief look into the savage universe of eighteenth century robbery yet in addition improved how we might interpret the financial ties between the Old World, the New World, and the African mainland during the Time of Investigation.

In the freezing waters of the Canadian Cold, the quest for the slippery Franklin Endeavor vessels — HMS Erebus and HMS Fear — enamored the world for quite a long time. The bound campaign drove by Sir John Franklin in 1845 expected to find the Northwest Entry yet met a lamentable end as the boats became icebound. The mission to track down these lost vessels, very much protected in the chilly Icy waters, turned into an image of diligence and coordinated effort among travelers, archeologists, and native networks. The disclosure of HMS Erebus in 2014 and HMS Fear in 2016 denoted a noteworthy second, disentangling the secrets encompassing the last days of the Franklin Endeavor and the circumstances looked by the group in their frantic battle for endurance.

One more oceanic riddle lies in the profundities off the bank of North Carolina — the disaster area of the USS Screen, an imaginative ironclad warship of the Nationwide conflict time. Participating in the renowned Skirmish of Hampton Streets against the Confederate ironclad CSS Virginia in 1862, the USS Screen sank during a tempest soon thereafter. Found in 1973, the disaster area gave priceless experiences into maritime fighting during an extraordinary period in military history. The famous rotating turret and different curios recuperated from the site featured the mechanical headways of the time and the essential pretended by ironclads in reshaping maritime fighting.

Digging into the later past, the destruction of the SS Thistlegorm in the Red Ocean is a demonstration of the hazards of wartime sea transport. Sunk by German planes in 1941 while conveying supplies for English soldiers, the SS Thistlegorm stays a submerged time container displaying the freight of war hardware, vehicles, and ordinary things frozen in time. Found by Jacques Cousteau during the 1950s, the site has turned into a famous objective for jumpers trying to investigate a cut of The Second Great War history laying on the sea floor.

The appeal of popular wrecks and lost vessels reaches out past the authentic and archeological aspects to embrace the human stories, mechanical progressions, and social associations that these lowered time cases address. The continuous investigation of these submerged secrets advances how we might interpret the past as well as fills our aggregate interest in the obscure domains of the world's seas. As innovation proceeds to progress and investigation methods develop, the charm of sea secrets stays a powerful power, motivating people in the future to wander into the somewhere down in quest for buried stories ready to be uncovered.

1.3 The challenges and significance of exploring the ocean depths to unlock these maritime secrets.

The Difficulties and Meaning of Investigating the Sea Profundities to Open Sea Insider facts

The investigation of the sea profundities, a domain that is more than 66% of the World's surface, is an undertaking loaded with difficulties and intricacies. However, the appeal of opening oceanic mysteries concealed underneath the waves has driven researchers, adventurers, and analysts to push the limits of human information. As we dive into the difficulties related with investigating the sea profundities, it becomes clear that the meaning of this pursuit reaches out a long ways past simple interest — it holds the keys to disentangling the secrets of our planet's past, present, and future.

One of the premier difficulties in investigating the sea profundities lies in the super natural circumstances that win underneath the surface. The devastating tensions applied by the heaviness of the water segment increment with profundity, arriving at levels that present critical dangers to both human jumpers and hardware. In the deep profundities, where tensions can surpass multiple times that at the surface, conventional investigation strategies are delivered illogical. To address this test, submarines, remotely worked vehicles (ROVs), and independent submerged vehicles (AUVs) have become irreplaceable devices, permitting specialists to explore the brutal circumstances and arrive at profundities that were once distant.

The interminable haziness of the remote ocean presents another impressive test. Daylight, the essential wellspring of light for the world's seas, is consumed by the water inside the initial not many hundred meters. Past this point, the sea plunges into unending murkiness. This shortfall of normal light confounds visual investigation and requires the utilization of cutting edge imaging innovations, for example, sonar and extreme focus lights, to catch clear pictures of the submerged territory. The advancement of refined camera frameworks and sonar innovation has been instrumental in beating the difficulties presented by the remote ocean's dark territories.

Notwithstanding the actual difficulties, the limitlessness of the sea presents a strategic and monetary obstacle to investigation endeavors. The region of the sea floor, quite a bit of which stays strange, requires careful wanting to enhance investigation courses and target explicit areas of premium. The expenses related with conveying and keeping up with cutting edge marine innovation, leading exploration endeavors, and it are significant to dissect gathered information. Global joint effort and organizations between research establishments, government organizations, and confidential substances are critical to pooling assets and aptitude, guaranteeing the progress of remote ocean investigation missions.

Investigating the sea profundities additionally presents moral contemplations, especially concerning the protection of submerged social legacy locales, like wrecks. The charm of significant relics has prompted cases of plundering and the unapproved expulsion of authentic things from lowered wrecks. The need to work out some kind of harmony between logical request and capable preservation has provoked the foundation of peaceful accords and rules, like the UNESCO Show on the Assurance of the Submerged Social Legacy. These systems expect to shield the respectability of submerged archeological destinations and advance moral practices in the review and safeguarding of lowered social legacy.

In spite of these difficulties, the meaning of investigating the sea profundities to open oceanic mysteries couldn't possibly be more significant. The lowered scenes harbor an abundance of verifiable, archeological, and logical information that holds the possibility to reshape how we might interpret the world. Wrecks, frequently alluded to as time containers of the past, give an immediate connection to oceanic history, offering bits of knowledge into maritime design, shipping lanes, and the human stories that unfurled on board these vessels. The investigation of wrecks enhances verifiable accounts as well as adds to how we might interpret innovative progressions, social trades, and the monetary ties that impacted social orders across various periods.

The geographical highlights concealed underneath the waves hold their own importance in unwinding the secrets of the World's internal activities. Submerged volcanoes, aqueous vents, and remote ocean channels give looks into the powerful cycles that administer the planet's development. Concentrating on these elements improves our appreciation of plate tectonics, mineral developments, and the interconnectedness of the World's geologic frameworks. The information got from these investigations has suggestions for logical examination as well as for grasping normal dangers, asset the board, and the more extensive setting of natural maintainability.

According to an organic viewpoint, the sea profundities harbor biological systems that oppose regular comprehension. The unusual and extraordinary animals adjusted to make due in outrageous circumstances offer important bits of knowledge into the flexibility of life on The planet. Bioluminescent organic entities that produce their own light without daylight, for instance, challenge biases about the restrictions of life in the most obscure corners of the sea. Concentrating on these extraordinary living things adds to how we might interpret biodiversity, biological connections, and the potential for life in outrageous conditions — an area of expanding interest in the quest for extraterrestrial territories.

Moreover, the sea profundities assume a critical part in directing the World's environment, making the investigation of these locales essential for environment science. The investigation of sea flows, temperature varieties, and substance arrangements in the remote ocean gives basic information to environment models and expectations. The sea goes about as a huge supply that ingests and reallocates heat, impacting weather conditions and environment conditions.

Opening the privileged insights of the sea profundities upgrades our capacity to resolve squeezing natural issues, execute feasible practices, and moderate the effects of environmental change.

With regards to mechanical development, the difficulties presented by remote ocean investigation drive progressions in marine innovation and designing. The advancement of submarines, ROVs, and AUVs with expanded capacities permits scientists to get to more noteworthy profundities and gather more exact information. The marriage of state of the art innovation and logical request pushes the limits of investigation as well as adds to the more extensive field of advanced mechanics, materials science, and information examination. The information acquired from remote ocean investigation advises the plan and improvement regarding submerged vehicles, sensors, and correspondence frameworks, with likely applications in fields past oceanography.

The investigation of the sea profundities isn't simply a logical pursuit — it is a fundamental part of mankind's more extensive mission for information and understanding. As we open oceanic privileged insights concealed underneath the waves, we gain a more profound appreciation for the interconnectedness of our planet and the perplexing connections that shape its different biological systems. The meaning of remote ocean investigation reaches out past the scholarly domain to motivate stunningness and marvel, cultivating a feeling of stewardship for the seas and a promise to safeguarding these basic environments for people in the future.

The difficulties and meaning of investigating the sea profundities stretch out into the domains of oceanography, a field that tries to disentangle the secrets of the oceans' physical, compound, and organic cycles. The tremendousness of the sea presents difficulties to gathering extensive information, and the outrageous states of the remote ocean entangle the estimation of basic boundaries. Understanding the sea's job in environment guideline, carbon cycling, and marine biodiversity requires careful perception and information assortment.

Sea flows, a central part of the World's environment framework, stay a point of convergence of oceanographic research. Remote ocean investigation permits researchers to concentrate on the mind boggling examples and elements of these flows, which assume a pivotal part in reallocating heat all over the planet. The Agulhas Flow, for example, impacts environment and atmospheric conditions in the Indian Sea, affecting local biological systems and fisheries. By disentangling the complexities of sea flows, specialists gain bits of knowledge into the components that administer environment fluctuation and add to the refinement of environment models.

Temperature varieties in the sea profundities are similarly basic to grasping environment elements. The remote ocean goes about as a repository that ingests and stores heat over extensive stretches, impacting the World's general energy balance.

Concentrating on temperature slopes in the deep profundities adds to environment science by giving information on warm extension — a main consideration in ocean level ascent. The investigation of sea profundities permits researchers to send particular sensors and instruments that action temperature profiles, working with a more far reaching comprehension of the sea's job in the worldwide environment framework.

Compound pieces in the remote ocean hold hints to the beginning of life, the advancement of marine environments, and the effects of human exercises. The investigation of submerged volcanoes and aqueous vents, where mineral-rich liquids connect with seawater, reveals insight into the geochemical processes that shape the sea floor. The special circumstances encompassing these elements make natural surroundings for extremophiles — creatures adjusted to get by in outrageous conditions. The revelation of these living things extends how we might interpret the potential for life in extraterrestrial conditions, adding to astrobiology and the quest for tenable zones past Earth.

Besides, the meaning of investigating the sea profundities stretches out to the carbon cycle — a central interaction that manages climatic carbon dioxide levels. The remote ocean goes about as an immense carbon sink, retaining and sequestering carbon through organic and actual cycles. Remote ocean creatures assume an essential part in carbon spinning through cycles like marine snow development, where natural particles sink to the sea floor. The investigation of these remote ocean biological systems gives important information to grasping the complicated trap of collaborations that impact the World's carbon spending plan.

Past physical and compound cycles, the biodiversity of the sea profundities addresses a logical boondocks that holds enormous importance for marine nature. The outrageous states of the remote ocean, portrayed by low temperatures, high tensions, and restricted food assets, challenge the versatility of marine life. However, the investigation of aqueous vent biological systems has uncovered a rich variety of animal categories exceptionally adjusted to flourish in these unforgiving conditions. From monster tube worms to eyeless shrimp, the occupants of the remote ocean offer experiences into the restrictions of life on The planet and the systems that drive transformative variations.

The meaning of remote ocean investigation additionally reaches out to the potential for biotechnological revelations. Remote ocean living beings, outfitted with transformations to endure outrageous circumstances, produce bioactive mixtures with remarkable properties. These mixtures have applications in medication, drugs, and materials science. Catalysts from extremophiles, for instance, have been saddled for modern cycles, while bioactive mixtures from remote ocean creatures show guarantee in drug improvement. The investigation of marine biotechnology in the sea profundities grows our insight into biodiversity as well as offers functional applications with suggestions for human wellbeing and industry.

As we dive further into the sea's secrets, the difficulties of investigating the deep profundities feature the requirement for manageable practices and capable stewardship of the marine climate. The fragile equilibrium of remote ocean environments, frequently described by sluggish paces of recuperation, requires cautious thought in the preparation and execution of investigation missions. The likely effect of human exercises, for example, remote ocean mining and asset extraction, highlights the significance of global participation and the advancement of administrative structures to moderate natural dangers.

The meaning of remote ocean investigation even with environmental change couldn't possibly be more significant. The sea, as a significant part of the World's environment framework, is encountering remarkable changes, including climbing temperatures, sea fermentation, and modifications available for use designs. Remote ocean investigation gives basic information to observing and figuring out these changes, offering bits of knowledge into the effects on marine environments and the more extensive ramifications for worldwide environment solidness. As the impacts of environmental change heighten, the sea profundities become a vital field for logical request, directing endeavors to adjust and relieve the outcomes of a warming planet.

With regards to mechanical development, the difficulties presented by remote ocean investigation drive progressions in marine innovation and designing. The advancement of subs, ROVs, and AUVs with expanded abilities permits analysts to get to more noteworthy profundities and gather more exact information. The marriage of state of the art innovation and logical request pushes the limits of investigation as well as adds to the more extensive field of mechanical technology, materials science, and information examination. The information acquired from remote ocean investigation advises the plan and improvement regarding submerged vehicles, sensors, and correspondence frameworks, with expected applications in fields past oceanography.

The difficulties and meaning of investigating the sea profundities to open oceanic insider facts structure a diverse story that ranges logical, ecological, mechanical, and moral aspects. The investigation of wrecks, geographical highlights, and environments concealed underneath the waves adds to how we might interpret history, Earth's geologic cycles, biodiversity, and the complicated elements of the worldwide environment framework. The determined quest for information in the deep profundities requires imaginative innovations, global joint effort, and a pledge to moral investigation rehearses. As humankind keeps on divulging the secrets of the sea, the meaning of remote ocean investigation will endure, offering a door to a more profound comprehension of our planet and the interconnected frameworks that shape its past, present, and future.

Chapter 2

The Franklin Expedition
Arctic Perils

The Franklin Campaign: Icy Dangers

The Franklin Campaign, quite possibly of the most prestigious and doomed adventure in the records of Cold investigation, remains as a demonstration of the risks of exploring the frosty waters of the Canadian Icy Archipelago. Driven by Sir John Franklin, a carefully prepared English maritime official, the undertaking expected to find the Northwest Entry — a legendary ocean course interfacing the Atlantic and Pacific Seas through the Icy. In any case, the journey, which set forth in 1845 with two boats, HMS Erebus and HMS Fear, finished in misfortune, leaving a getting through secret that would spellbind pilgrims, students of history, and general society for over 100 years.

The Icy, with its brutal and unforgiving circumstances, presented imposing difficulties to the Franklin Campaign all along. The boats were extraordinarily supported with iron plating to endure the strain of ice, and arrangements were amassed for a lengthy excursion. Notwithstanding, the cruel truth of Cold investigation would before long appear in a progression of catastrophes that unfurled, fixing the destiny of the campaign and its group.

The journey initiated with high expectations and assumptions. Franklin, a regarded and experienced voyager, was shared with the mission with cross the Northwest Entry — an essential stream that held the commitment of more limited shipping lanes and expanded oceanic access. In any case, the Icy, with its erratic climate, moving ice floes, and tricky circumstances, introduced difficulties that outperformed the mechanical and navigational capacities of the time.

As the campaign wandered into unknown waters, it became trapped in the ice of Victoria Waterway, close to Lord William Island. The boats, at first caught in the frozen ocean, demonstrated unfit to explore right out of the frigid hold. The group confronted the brutal truth of being icebound for a drawn out period, defying the double difficulties of outrageous cold and restricted assets. The Icy climate, with its interminable dimness throughout the cold weather months, added a mental cost to the actual difficulties persevered by the team.

The underlying idealism of the Franklin Undertaking before long gave way to urgency. While trying to find help, Sir John Franklin and a portion of his men set out by walking in 1847, abandoning the boats. Unfortunately, the unforgiving Cold circumstances killed Franklin and a few others, adding to the mounting cost of the undertaking. With the administration in chaos, the leftover team confronted a desperate circumstance, caught in the frigid limits of the Icy wild.

The quest for the Northwest Entry had changed into a battle for endurance. The group confronted a shortage of food, lessening supplies, and the persevering infringement of the Icy winter. Forsaking the boats, the survivors endeavored to travel overland, looking for salvage and help from the unwelcoming Icy scene. Be that as it may, the excursion demonstrated dangerous, with many surrendering to openness, starvation, and illness.

The destiny of the Franklin Campaign remained covered in secret for a really long time, provoking various hunt endeavors and investigations into the conditions encompassing the misfortune. The absence of correspondence or sightings of the campaign energized hypothesis and fables, leading to stories of savagery, franticness, and experiences with legendary animals. The obscure destiny of the team turned into an unpleasant story that waited in the aggregate creative mind, changing the Franklin Campaign into an image of both the charm and the dangers of Icy investigation.

It was only after 1859 that the main unmistakable signs to the destiny of the Franklin Campaign were found. An inquiry endeavor drove by Sir Francis McClintock found a cairn on Lord William Island containing a note recording the relinquishment of the boats and the passing of Franklin and a few group individuals. The note uncovered the troubling conditions looked by the endeavor, including the deficiency of the two boats and the choice to travel toward the south looking for help. In spite of this forward leap, many inquiries stayed unanswered, and the specific area of the submerged boats stayed a secret.

The quest for the missing vessels picked up reestablished speed in the twentieth 100 years, powered by progresses in innovation and a relentless longing to unwind the mysteries of the Franklin Campaign. In 2014 and 2016, the two HMS Erebus and HMS Fear were at long last found on the Cold seabed by the Parks Canada-drove Victoria Waterway Endeavor. The very much protected wrecks gave an abundance of data, revealing insight into the last snapshots of the endeavor and offering experiences into the difficulties looked by the team.

The disclosures of the submerged boats carried conclusion to the persevering through secret of the Franklin Endeavor, however they additionally brought up new issues. The surprisingly very much saved state of the disaster areas alluded to the brutal circumstances looked by the team, including openness to lead harming from ineffectively safeguarded canned merchandise. The disaster area of HMS Erebus, specifically, uncovered relics and individual things that gave a piercing look into the day to day routines of the ones who left on the doomed excursion.

The Franklin Campaign, while shocking, has made a permanent imprint on the historical backdrop of Icy investigation. The risks looked by the group highlight the imposing difficulties of exploring the frosty waters of the Canadian Icy Archipelago — a district that remaining parts among the most ungracious and unforgiving on The planet. The charm of finding the Northwest Entry, driven by dreams of shipping lanes and sea access, slammed into the brutal real factors of the Icy climate, prompting an adventure of franticness, endurance, and eventually, misfortune.

The meaning of the Franklin Endeavor reaches out past the verifiable story, digging into the domains of antiquarianism, humanities, and natural science. The disclosures of the submerged boats and the curios they contain offer a substantial connection to the past, giving a brief look into the existences of the ones who set out on the disastrous excursion. The disaster area destinations, presently safeguarded as public notable locales, act as submerged exhibition halls that add to how we might interpret sea history and the difficulties presented by Icy investigation.

According to a natural point of view, the Cold locale possessed by the Franklin Undertaking has gone through massive changes in late many years. The warming environment has prompted the retreat of ocean ice, changing the elements of the Cold biological system. The disclosures of the submerged boats and the continuous examination in the area contribute important information for understanding the effects of environmental change on the Icy climate, remembering its belongings for ice cover, ocean levels, and marine biological systems.

The Franklin Endeavor, with its story of desire, misfortune, and misfortune, resounds as a preventative section throughout the entire existence of investigation. It fills in as a sign of the sensitive harmony between human undertakings and the considerable powers of nature.

The appeal of the obscure, encapsulated in the mission for the Northwest Entry, conflicted with the brutal real factors of the Icy climate, passing on a getting through heritage that keeps on catching the creative mind of those attracted to the investigation of Earth's most remote and testing scenes.

The Franklin Campaign's inheritance reaches out past the Cold dangers and unfortunate destiny of its group, diving into the unpredictable woven artwork of sea investigation, mechanical development, and the getting through human soul that drives globe-trotters into unknown domains. The charm of finding the Northwest Section, a fantasy held onto for quite a long time, typified the mission for new outskirts and the commitment of opening monetary and competitive edges. The Franklin Campaign, while damaged by hardship, added to the more extensive account of Icy investigation and the tireless quest for information that characterizes the human experience.

The nineteenth century saw a flood in Cold investigation as countries looked for elective shipping lanes and navigational sections. The quest for the Northwest Entry, a speculative ocean course interfacing the Atlantic and Pacific Seas through the Icy archipelago, turned into an image of investigation and international desire. The Franklin Undertaking, authorized by the English Admiral's office, was important for this bigger work to diagram obscure waters and attest strength in the race for sea matchless quality. The risks looked by the undertaking highlighted the imposing difficulties inborn in wandering into the cold domains of the Canadian Icy.

The mechanical developments of the time, albeit earth shattering, were inadequate to beat the unforgiving states of the Icy. The boats, HMS Erebus and HMS Dread, were built up with iron plating to endure the tension of ice, and steam motors were introduced to enhance conventional sail power. Nonetheless, these progressions demonstrated lacking against the steady hold of the Icy ice. The mission for a traversable Northwest Entry requested boldness and assurance as well as a mechanical jump that would just come in resulting a very long time with headways in icebreaker innovation and route.

The grievous destiny of the Franklin Undertaking likewise highlights the mental and close to home cost of Icy investigation. The team confronted a long time of haziness, outrageous cold, and seclusion — a blend that tried the constraints of human perseverance. As the icebound boats turned into a jail, the team wrestled with waning supplies, the ghost of scurvy, and the difficulties of keeping up with confidence notwithstanding apparently outlandish chances. The unforgiving real factors of endurance in the Icy wild were intensified by the psychological type of vulnerability, prompting urgency and heartbreaking choices.

The persevering through secret of the Franklin Campaign caught the public creative mind and energized various inquiry endeavors throughout the long term. The mission to disentangle the destiny of Sir John Franklin and his team turned into an image of strength, persistence, and the human soul's dauntless will to look for replies notwithstanding difficulty.

The secret enlivened writing, workmanship, and innumerable undertakings devoted to revealing reality. The tireless quest for information and conclusion mirrored the more extensive human impulse to face the obscure and enlighten the shadows of vulnerability.

The revelations of HMS Erebus and HMS Dread in 2014 and 2016 denoted a defining moment in the Franklin Campaign's story. The surprisingly very much saved wrecks gave a substantial association with the past, offering a brief look into the regular routines, schedules, and difficulties looked by the team. The curios recuperated from the disaster areas, including individual things, navigational instruments, and arrangements, gave a piercing connect to the human stories that unfurled in the midst of the Cold dangers. The submerged locales became archeological fortunes, uncovering bits of knowledge into nineteenth century maritime innovation, investigation rehearses, and the effect of Cold circumstances on materials and designs.

The natural setting of the Franklin Campaign adds one more layer of importance to its story. The Cold, a district going through fast environmental change, fills in as an impactful scenery to the difficulties looked by Franklin and his group. The warming temperatures and decreasing ocean ice in the 21st century add to the advancing Cold account. The disclosures of the submerged boats offer an exceptional chance to concentrate on the ecological changes in the locale after some time, giving important information to environment researchers and natural specialists. The disaster areas act as time containers, epitomizing the at various times states of the Cold climate.

The Franklin Campaign, while a misfortune, addresses a vital turning point in the more extensive history of Cold investigation. It fills in as a useful example about the fragile harmony between human desire and the imposing powers of nature. The mission for the Northwest Entry, driven by monetary, international, and logical thought processes, slammed into the brutal real factors of the Cold climate, bringing about a part of investigation set apart by both accomplishment and significant misfortune. The tradition of the Franklin Undertaking perseveres as a standard for figuring out the intricacies of investigation, the dauntless human soul, and the continuous difficulties of exploring Earth's most outrageous conditions.

The effect of the Franklin Campaign on the comprehension of Icy investigation resounds in contemporary talk. The tale of the disastrous excursion fills in as a focal point through which to look at the morals of investigation, the connection among mankind and the normal world, and the examples gained from the risks looked by Franklin and his team. As current investigation wanders into new outskirts, including the profundities of the sea and the investigation of different planets, the reverberations of the Franklin Endeavor's difficulties and accomplishments stay significant.

The Franklin Campaign's Icy dangers, terrible destiny, and ensuing disclosures exemplify the substance of investigation — a pursuit that envelops human desire, the journey for information, and the strength to defy the unexplored world. The charm of the Northwest Entry, driven by dreams of oceanic shipping lanes and monetary benefit, slammed into the brutal real factors of the Icy climate, bringing about an adventure that resounds across hundreds of years. The Franklin Campaign remains as a demonstration of the dauntless soul of investigation, the intricacies of human undertakings, and the continuous mission to grasp the secrets of our planet. In the investigation of Earth's most remote and testing scenes, the tradition of the Franklin Undertaking keeps on molding how we might interpret the human limit with respect to both victory and misfortune.

2.1 Detailed exploration of the ill-fated Franklin Expedition in search of the Northwest Passage.

The Disastrous Franklin Endeavor: Misfortune in the Quest for the Northwest Section

The nineteenth century saw an intense journey for the tricky Northwest Entry — a legendary ocean course connecting the Atlantic and Pacific Seas through the Icy. This quest for a traversable easy route held the commitment of monetary benefits, more limited shipping lanes, and expanded oceanic access. At the focal point of this desire was the disastrous Franklin Campaign, a lamentable part in the chronicles of Icy investigation that unfurled against the background of impressive difficulties, mechanical impediments, and the unforgiving real factors of the Icy climate.

In 1845, Sir John Franklin, a carefully prepared English maritime official and experienced Icy wayfarer, was endowed with the order of a campaign that meant to cross the Northwest Entry. Two boats, HMS Erebus and HMS Fear, were chosen for this risky excursion. The campaign set forth from Britain with high expectations, energized by a mix of oceanic mastery, mechanical development, and the unyielding soul of investigation. In any case, the Icy, with its flighty climate, moving ice floes, and slippery circumstances, would before long end up being an unforgiving enemy.

The mechanical headways of the time, however significant, were deficient to defeat the difficulties presented by the Cold climate. The boats were furnished with supported iron plating to endure the tensions of ice, and steam motors were integrated to enhance customary sail power. Regardless of these developments, the innovation of the mid-nineteenth century missed the mark even with the unforgiving real factors of Cold investigation. The group confronted the dangers of exploring tricky waters as well as the mental cost of detachment, never-ending murkiness, and the persevering infringement of the Cold winter.

As the Franklin Endeavor wandered into strange waters, it experienced the frosty hold of Victoria Waterway, close to Ruler William Island. The boats became caught in the frozen ocean, unfit to explore right out of the frosty maze.

The group stood up to the unforgiving truth of being icebound — a circumstance that would present difficult difficulties to their endurance. The Icy, with its gnawing cold and ruined scene, changed the journey for the Northwest Section into a fight for endurance against nature's impressive powers.

The group confronted a shortage of food, waning supplies, and the mental cost of drawn out detachment. The boats, at first planned as vessels of investigation, became jails in the cold wild. The Cold winter, with its a long time of never-ending obscurity, added a layer of difficulty that tried the constraints of human perseverance. In spite of the underlying confidence, the Franklin Campaign before long dropped into a frantic battle for endurance, set apart by disease, openness, and the dismal acknowledgment that the undertaking's targets had become optional to the quick requirement for food and warmth.

In a frantic bid to look for help, Sir John Franklin and a portion of his men set out by walking in 1847, abandoning the boats. Sadly, the unforgiving Icy circumstances killed Franklin and a few others, adding to the mounting cost of the undertaking. With the initiative in disorder, the excess team confronted a desperate circumstance, caught in the frozen region of the Cold wild. Leaving the boats, the survivors endeavored to travel overland, looking for salvage and help from the unwelcoming climate. Nonetheless, the excursion demonstrated dangerous, with many surrendering to openness, starvation, and infection.

The destiny of the Franklin Endeavor remained covered in secret for a really long time, provoking various hunt endeavors and investigations into the conditions encompassing the misfortune. The absence of correspondence or sightings of the undertaking energized hypothesis and legends, bringing about stories of barbarianism, frenzy, and experiences with legendary animals. The obscure destiny of the team turned into an unpleasant story that waited in the aggregate creative mind, changing the Franklin Undertaking into an image of both the charm and the risks of Cold investigation.

It was only after 1859 that the main unmistakable hints to the destiny of the Franklin Undertaking were found. A pursuit campaign drove by Sir Francis McClintock found a cairn on Lord William Island containing a note reporting the surrender of the boats and the demise of Franklin and a few team individuals. The note uncovered the terrible conditions looked by the campaign, including the deficiency of the two boats and the choice to travel toward the south looking for help. In spite of this leap forward, many inquiries stayed unanswered, and the specific area of the submerged boats stayed a secret.

The quest for the missing vessels picked up recharged speed in the twentieth 100 years, energized by propels in innovation and a steady longing to disentangle the mysteries of the Franklin Endeavor. In 2014 and 2016, the two HMS Erebus and HMS Fear were at last found on the Cold seabed by the Parks Canada-drove Victoria Waterway Campaign.

The very much protected wrecks gave an abundance of data, revealing insight into the last snapshots of the endeavor and offering bits of knowledge into the difficulties looked by the group.

The revelations of the submerged boats carried conclusion to the persevering through secret of the Franklin Campaign, however they likewise brought up new issues. The strikingly all around saved state of the disaster areas indicated the unforgiving circumstances looked by the group, including openness to lead harming from inadequately safeguarded canned products. The disaster area of HMS Erebus, specifically, uncovered curios and individual things that gave a powerful look into the day to day routines of the ones who set out on the doomed excursion.

The Franklin Endeavor, while grievous, has made a permanent imprint on the historical backdrop of Icy investigation. The hazards looked by the group highlight the imposing difficulties of exploring the cold waters of the Canadian Icy Archipelago — a locale that remaining parts among the most unfriendly and unforgiving on The planet. The charm of finding the Northwest Section, driven by dreams of shipping lanes and oceanic access, slammed into the cruel real factors of the Icy climate, prompting an adventure of urgency, endurance, and eventually, misfortune.

The meaning of the Franklin Endeavor reaches out past the authentic account, diving into the domains of archaic exploration, human studies, and ecological science. The disclosures of the submerged boats and the curios they contain offer an unmistakable connection to the past, giving a brief look into the existences of the ones who left on the doomed excursion. The disaster area locales, presently safeguarded as public notable destinations, act as submerged historical centers that add to how we might interpret sea history and the difficulties presented by Icy investigation.

According to a natural viewpoint, the Cold district possessed by the Franklin Campaign has gone through huge changes in ongoing many years. The warming environment has prompted the retreat of ocean ice, changing the elements of the Icy biological system. The disclosures of the submerged boats and the continuous examination in the locale contribute significant information for understanding the effects of environmental change on the Cold climate, remembering its belongings for ice cover, ocean levels, and marine biological systems.

The Franklin Undertaking, while a misfortune, addresses a vital crossroads in the more extensive history of Cold investigation. It fills in as a wake up call about the fragile harmony between human desire and the imposing powers of nature. The journey for the Northwest Entry, driven by financial, international, and logical thought processes, crashed into the cruel real factors of the Cold climate, bringing about a section of investigation set apart by both accomplishment and significant misfortune. The tradition of the Franklin Campaign perseveres as a standard for figuring out the intricacies of investigation, the dauntless human soul, and the continuous difficulties of exploring Earth's most outrageous conditions.

The effect of the Franklin Undertaking on the comprehension of Icy investigation resounds in contemporary talk. The narrative of the disastrous excursion fills in as a focal point through which to look at the morals of investigation, the connection among mankind and the normal world, and the illustrations gained from the dangers looked by Franklin and his team. As current investigation wanders into new boondocks, including the profundities of the sea and the investigation of different planets, the reverberations of the Franklin Undertaking's difficulties and accomplishments stay important.

The Franklin Undertaking, regardless of its sad end, holds persevering through importance in the more extensive setting of investigation, oceanic history, and the human journey for information. The doomed excursion fills in as a wake up call about the intrinsic dangers of wandering into obscure and outrageous conditions, featuring the fragile harmony among desire and the impressive powers of nature.

The charm of the Northwest Section, a fantasy that dazzled travelers for a really long time, was profoundly interlaced with monetary and international desires. European powers looked for an immediate shipping lane to Asia that would sidestep the extensive and dangerous excursion around the southern tip of South America or the Cape of Good Expectation. The commitment of a traversable entry through the Icy archipelago tempt the minds of countries competing for predominance in worldwide exchange. The Franklin Undertaking, endorsed by the English Admiral's office, addressed a critical interest in this fantastic vision of sea investigation.

In any case, the Cold, with its cruel circumstances and erratic nature, presented difficulties that rose above the mechanical abilities of the time. The boats, however furnished with cutting edge developments for the period, were poorly ready to endure the determined hold of the ice. The iron plating intended to safeguard against ice strain might have added to the boats' weakness, as it made them more helpless to harm from moving ice. The steam motors, intended to aid impetus, demonstrated unfeasible in the frigid waters and drank valuable coal saves. These mechanical constraints highlight the colossal challenges looked by the team as they explored the slippery waters of the Canadian Icy.

The mental cost of the Cold climate on the team of the Franklin Campaign is an impactful part of the misfortune. Drawn out detachment, unending obscurity, and the unforgiving states of the Icy winter added layers of difficulty that tried the constraints of human perseverance. The boats, at first expected as vessels of investigation and disclosure, changed into binding spaces that exacerbated the group's battle for endurance. The psychological kind of vulnerability and the frantic mission for food and warmth made a nerve racking story of distress and misfortune.

The choice by Sir John Franklin and a portion of his men to forsake the boats looking for help denoted a critical second in the undertaking's disentangling. The brutal Icy circumstances killed Franklin and others, leaving the excess team in a desperate circumstance.

The resulting endeavor to travel overland looking for salvage prompted further fatalities, as openness, starvation, and sickness incurred significant damage. The tale of the Franklin Undertaking, with its components of initiative difficulties, urgency, and heartbreaking decisions, turned into a mind boggling story that unfurled against the unmistakable background of the Icy wild.

The secret encompassing the destiny of the Franklin Undertaking energized various quest endeavors and dazzled the public creative mind for quite a long time. The absence of definitive proof, joined with stories of barbarianism and extraordinary experiences, changed the story into an unpleasant legend. The journey for the missing boats became a mission to disentangle verifiable secrets as well as an emblematic excursion into the obscure, mirroring humankind's unquenchable interest and the persevering through charm of investigation.

The disclosures of HMS Erebus and HMS Fear in 2014 and 2016 added another section to the account of the Franklin Endeavor. The surprisingly very much saved wrecks gave a substantial connection to the past, permitting specialists and students of history to acquire exceptional experiences into the circumstances looked by the group. The curios recuperated from the disaster areas, including individual things, navigational instruments, and arrangements, made a strong association with the human stories that unfurled in the midst of the Cold risks. The submerged destinations, safeguarded as public memorable locales, act as time containers that add to how we might interpret nineteenth century maritime innovation, investigation rehearses, and the effect of Icy circumstances on materials and designs.

The ecological setting of the Franklin Undertaking is one more layer that adds profundity to its importance. The Cold area, where the doomed excursion unfurled, has gone through significant changes in ongoing a very long time because of environmental change. The warming temperatures, retreat of ocean ice, and changes in marine biological systems have changed the Icy scene. The revelations of the submerged boats offer an extraordinary chance to concentrate on the natural changes in the locale over the long run, giving important information to environment researchers and ecological scientists.

The tradition of the Franklin Undertaking perseveres through as a wake up call as well as an image of flexibility, industriousness, and the human soul's constant quest for information. The mission for the Northwest Section, while set apart by misfortune, addresses a part in the excellent story of investigation that traverses hundreds of years. The Franklin Undertaking's difficulties and extreme destiny mirror the complex interaction between human aspiration, the regular world, and the unusual elements of investigation.

In contemporary talk, the Franklin Endeavor fills in as a standard for conversations on investigation morals, natural stewardship, and the obligations of wandering into remote and delicate biological systems.

As present day investigation wanders into new wildernesses, from the profundities of the sea to the investigation of different planets, the examples gained from the Franklin Endeavor stay significant. The fragile harmony between logical interest and ecological effect requires smart thought and capable investigation rehearses.

The disastrous Franklin Campaign, with its shocking end and resulting revelations, remains as a convincing section throughout the entire existence of investigation. The charm of the Northwest Section, driven by monetary and international desires, slammed into the unforgiving real factors of the Cold climate, bringing about an adventure of urgency, endurance, and eventually, misfortune. The meaning of the endeavor reaches out past its verifiable story, enveloping mechanical development, mental versatility, ecological change, and the getting through human soul that endures notwithstanding misfortune. The Franklin Endeavor stays a permanent piece of the investigation heritage, welcoming reflection on the intricacies, challenges, and significant illustrations intrinsic chasing after the unexplored world.

2.2 The historical context and motivations behind the expedition.

The Franklin Campaign, a urgent section in the chronicles of Cold investigation, unfurled against a setting of verifiable setting, international desires, and the mission for the slippery Northwest Entry. The mid-nineteenth century was set apart by an intense craving among European powers to find a safe easy route that would interface the Atlantic and Pacific Seas through the Cold archipelago. This fantasy, powered by monetary impetuses and international rivalry, established the ground-work for the disastrous Franklin Undertaking.

The nineteenth century was a period of incredible oceanic investigation, driven by a conjunction of monetary, logical, and key thought processes. The Modern Upset had introduced a time of extraordinary innovative progressions, changing social orders and economies. With the expanded abilities of steam power and iron-clad boats, countries looked for new shipping lanes that would work with quicker and more proficient associations between their domains and worldwide business sectors. The journey for the Northwest Section, a legendary ocean course that guaranteed an easy route to the wealth of Asia, turned into a focal point of investigation tries.

The craving to find a traversable Northwest Entry was established in monetary contemplations as well as driven by international and key worries. European powers were taken part in extraordinary contest for provincial domains and world-wide impact. Having an immediate shipping lane through the Cold would give a critical benefit, empowering speedier admittance to the business sectors of Asia and improving a country's oceanic incomparability. The Northwest Section was viewed as a possible road for declaring strength in the worldwide exchange organization, and countries were anxious to put resources into campaigns that could open its mysteries.

In this unique situation, the English Office of the chief naval officer, under the authority of Sir John Pushcart, assumed a significant part in molding Icy investigation procedures. Pushcart, the Second Secretary to the Admiral's office, was a resolute supporter for Cold investigation and accepted that the revelation of the Northwest Section would get English predominance in world exchange. He effectively advanced Icy undertakings and upheld the foundation of the Regal Maritime Icy Campaign Asset, which gave monetary support to exploratory endeavors. The Franklin Undertaking arose as a lead try inside this more extensive system of English Icy investigation.

Sir John Franklin, a recognized maritime official with an abundance of Icy experience, was decided to lead the endeavor. Franklin's past processes, remembering his contribution for two overland undertakings in the Cold and his governorship of Van Diemen's Property (present-day Tasmania), showed the two his ability and flexibility. Franklin was viewed as a carefully prepared traveler who had the initiative characteristics considered fundamental for such a difficult mission. His choice mirrored the Office of the chief naval officer's obligation to endow the Northwest Section mission to an accomplished and competent authority.

In 1845, the Franklin Campaign set forth from Britain with two exceptionally prepared ships — HMS Erebus and HMS Fear. The boats were built up with iron plating to endure the tensions of ice, and their steam motors were expected to give assistant power in exploring through ice-plagued waters. The endeavor, comprising of 129 officials and team, conveyed arrangements for a lengthy excursion, expecting the difficulties of Cold investigation.

As the undertaking initiated, there was a demeanor of confidence and expectation. The team, including prepared mariners and officials, left on a mission that held the commitment of disclosure and win. People in general, as well, followed the endeavor with strong fascination, anxious to observe the unfurling show of Cold investigation and the expected disclosure of the long-looked for Northwest Section.

Notwithstanding, the Icy, with its flighty and cold circumstances, would before long uncover its considerable difficulties. The boats experienced the frosty hold of Victoria Waterway, close to Lord William Island, and became caught in the frozen ocean. The mechanical advancements of the time, while noteworthy, demonstrated deficient even with the Icy's persevering powers. The group ended up caught in the ice, and the underlying confidence of revelation gave way to the cruel truth of endurance in the frozen wild.

The verifiable setting of the Franklin Endeavor includes the mechanical and key viewpoints as well as the cultural and social components of nineteenth century investigation. The undertaking, with its terrific aspirations and sad end, became significant of the period's soul of disclosure, epitomizing the assurance to vanquish the obscure and extend the limits of human information. The interest with investigation was not just a logical undertaking but rather an impression of the more extensive yearnings and upsides of society during that period.

The unfurling misfortune of the Franklin Undertaking, with its untold difficulties and extreme secret, turned into an image that resounded a long ways past the Cold waters. The public's creative mind was charmed by the endeavor's journey for the Northwest Entry, and the vulnerability encompassing its destiny filled a feeling of wonderment and interest. The stories of Icy investigation, loaded down with chivalry, danger, and the obscure, dazzled the Victorian creative mind and added to a more extensive social folklore of investigation and disclosure.

The job of Sir John Cart and the English Admiral's office in forming Cold investigation procedures highlights the institutional and vital components of the Franklin Campaign. Cart's vision for English maritime strength and worldwide impact was personally attached to the effective disclosure of the Northwest Section. The Chief of naval operations' office's help, both monetary and calculated, highlighted the responsibility of the English government to put resources into investigation for of getting financial and upper hands on the world stage.

The verifiable setting of the Franklin Endeavor additionally crosses with the more extensive setting of nineteenth century dominion and expansionism. The mission for new shipping lanes and competitive edges was unpredictably connected to the supreme aspirations of European powers. The international rivalry for control of domains and assets, combined with the craving to affirm predominance in worldwide exchange, drove the investigation of far off and testing districts like the Cold.

The Franklin Campaign, in this sense, was a microcosm of the bigger international scene of the time.

The inspirations driving the campaign, while established in monetary and key goals, were likewise impacted by a feeling of logical interest and public pride. The disclosure of a safe Northwest Entry was viewed as an accomplishment that wouldn't just help exchange yet additionally raise the situation with the country that accomplished it. Logical investigation, combined with the longing to add to the more extensive comprehension of geology and environment, assumed a part in molding the undertaking's targets.

The people engaged with the Franklin Endeavor, from Sir John Franklin himself to the officials and group, addressed a cross-part of Victorian culture. The officials were frequently drawn from the positions of the Illustrious Naval force, mirroring a blend of oceanic mastery and military discipline. The team, containing mariners, sailors, and specialists, carried different abilities to the undertaking. The cooperative exertion expected for such an endeavor featured the interdisciplinary idea of Icy investigation.

The campaign's takeoff from Britain in 1845 denoted the perfection of long periods of arranging, arrangement, and expectation. The public's interest with Icy investigation, energized by prior undertakings and stories of polar experiences, added to the boundless premium in the Franklin Endeavor. The mission, with its reasonable goals and the accomplished initiative of Sir John Franklin, was seen as a stupendous endeavor that exemplified the soul of Victorian investigation.

As the endeavor unfurled, with the boats exploring through the Cold waters and confronting the difficulties of ice, the general population stayed drew in with the unfurling show. Insight about the undertaking's advancement, imparted through letters, reports, and periodic updates, increased the feeling of expectation. The Franklin Undertaking turned into a public undertaking, catching the minds of the people who followed its direction from the solace of their homes in England.

The verifiable setting of the Franklin Undertaking stretches out past the nineteenth hundred years and resounds into the current day. The journey for the Northwest Entry, when driven by monetary and international inspirations, presently meets with contemporary conversations on environmental change and its effect on the Cold district. The liquefying of ocean ice has opened additional opportunities for sea route through the Northwest Entry, reviving conversations on its key and monetary importance.

The inspirations that supported the Franklin Campaign were well established in the verifiable setting of nineteenth century investigation, where logical interest, monetary interests, and international goals merged. The mid-1800s were set apart by a feeling of investigation and mechanical development, with the Modern Unrest changing social orders and economies. Against this scenery, the journey for the Northwest Entry held significant ramifications for countries competing for worldwide strength.

The monetary inspirations driving the undertaking were attached to the intense longing for a more straightforward shipping lane to Asia. European powers looked for ways of avoiding the extensive and unsafe excursions around the southern tips of South America and Africa. The commitment of a traversable Northwest Entry, a more limited course through the Cold archipelago, enamored the creative mind of countries enthused about upgrading their sea shipping lanes. The potential financial advantages were monstrous, with the undertaking seen as a critical interest in getting a competitive edge in the worldwide exchange organization.

International contemplations assumed a critical part in molding the undertaking's targets. The journey for regional predominance and worldwide impact energized royal desires, and having command over a traversable Northwest Section was seen as an international benefit. The English Admiral's office, under the initiative of Sir John Hand truck, perceived the essential significance of the Icy district and effectively upheld Cold investigation for of getting English maritime matchless quality. The Franklin Undertaking, with its reasonable targets and experienced initiative, turned into a leader try inside the more extensive setting of English international technique.

Logical interest likewise added to the inspirations driving the campaign. The nineteenth century was set apart by a developing interest in the normal world, and investigation was viewed for of growing logical information. The longing to figure out the geology, environment, and normal assets of the Cold area drove the logical goals of the Franklin Undertaking.

The team included naturalists and researchers entrusted with recording and concentrating on the verdure, fauna, and geographical highlights experienced during the excursion. The campaign, in this manner, filled a double need — progressing logical comprehension while seeking after monetary and international objectives.

Sir John Franklin, decided to lead the campaign, encapsulated the qualities considered fundamental for such a difficult mission. His past encounters in Cold investigation, including overland endeavors and influential positions, went with him a characteristic decision. Franklin's governorship of Van Diemen's Property likewise showed authoritative abilities and flexibility. His determination mirrored the Admiral's office's acknowledgment of the requirement for an accomplished and strong commandant to explore the vulnerabilities of Icy investigation.

The group of the Franklin Campaign addressed a cross-part of Victorian culture. Officials were frequently drawn from the Imperial Naval force, consolidating sea ability with military discipline. The group included mariners, sailors, and specialists, each contributing extraordinary abilities to the endeavor's prosperity. The cooperative exertion expected for such an endeavor featured the interdisciplinary idea of Cold investigation, where maritime ability, logical information, and useful abilities were fundamental for endurance.

The public's interest with Cold investigation, filled by prior endeavors and stories of polar experiences, added to the boundless premium in the Franklin Campaign.

The mission, with its unmistakable goals and the accomplished initiative of Sir John Franklin, caught the Victorian creative mind as a fantastic endeavor that epitomized the soul of investigation. Fresh insight about the undertaking's advancement, conveyed through letters, reports, and infrequent updates, increased the feeling of expectation, and the Franklin Campaign turned into a public undertaking.

As the endeavor unfurled, the difficulties of exploring through frigid waters and confronting the brutal states of the Icy became evident. The boats, HMS Erebus and HMS Dread, outfitted with state of the art innovation for the time, experienced hardships in the unforgiving climate. The iron-plated bodies intended to endure ice strain might have added to the boats' weakness, and the steam motors expected for assistant power demonstrated unreasonable in cold waters. The innovative constraints of the mid-nineteenth century became clear as the team wrestled with the tireless hold of the Cold.

The group's mental and actual perseverance was tried as they went up against the cruel real factors of Icy investigation. Delayed seclusion, never-ending haziness, and the infringing Cold winter added layers of difficulty that stressed the constraints of human flexibility. The boats, at first imagined as vessels of revelation, became limiting spaces in the frozen wild. The psychological type of vulnerability and the frantic mission for food and warmth made a nerve racking story of distress and misfortune.

The choice by Sir John Franklin and some team individuals to forsake the boats looking for help denoted a vital second in the undertaking's unwinding. The brutal Icy circumstances guaranteed lives, including Franklin's, and the excess group confronted a desperate circumstance. The resulting endeavor to travel overland looking for salvage prompted further fatalities, as openness, starvation, and illness incurred significant damage. The Franklin Endeavor, when an image of investigation and desire, turned into a shocking adventure of endurance against nature's imposing powers.

The verifiable setting of the Franklin Undertaking stretches out past the nineteenth hundred years and reverberates with contemporary conversations on environmental change and the effect of human exercises on the Cold district. The journey for the Northwest Section, when driven by financial and international inspirations, crosses with present-day banters on ecological manageability and dependable investigation. The tradition of the Franklin Endeavor perseveres as a useful example, provoking reflection on the intricacies, challenges, and getting through charm of wandering into the obscure chasing information and revelation.

The inspirations driving the Franklin Campaign were complex, incorporating financial, key, logical, and social aspects. The campaign, arranged in the verifiable setting of nineteenth century investigation, mirrored the aspirations and upsides of Victorian culture. The journey for the Northwest Section, while driven by international contemplations and financial interests, additionally exemplified the soul of logical interest and public pride. The misfortune that came to pass for the undertaking, with its mechanical difficulties and human expenses, turned into an image of both the glory and the dangers of Icy investigation. The Franklin Undertaking's verifiable importance perseveres, inciting reflection on the mind boggling exchange between human desire, the regular world, and the getting through mission for information.

2.3 The discovery of HMS Erebus and HMS Terror and the technological advancements in marine archaeology.

The Disclosure of HMS Erebus and HMS Dread: A Sea Archeological Victory

The disclosure of HMS Erebus and HMS Dread denoted a turning point in the domain of sea paleontology, unwinding the secrets of the doomed Franklin Campaign that had escaped investigation for almost 170 years. In 2014 and 2016, the amazingly all around saved wrecks were found on the Cold seabed by the Parks Canada-drove Victoria Waterway Undertaking, carrying conclusion to perhaps of the most getting through oceanic secret ever.

The innovative headways that worked with this disclosure address an intermingling of state of the art marine paleontology, submerged investigation, and remote detecting advances. The meaning of the revelation stretches out past the authentic story of the Franklin Undertaking, offering experiences into the difficulties of Cold investigation, the safeguarding of submerged legacy, and the developing philosophies of marine paleontology.

The quest for the missing vessels picked up recharged speed in the 21st 100 years, driven by headways in innovation and a constant longing to open the mysteries of the Franklin Campaign. The utilization of best in class hardware, including side-examine sonar, remotely worked vehicles (ROVs), and independent submerged vehicles (AUVs), altered the way to deal with submerged investigation. These innovations permitted specialists to study immense region of the Cold seabed with remarkable detail, making a virtual guide of the submerged scene.

Side-examine sonar, specifically, assumed a urgent part in the disclosure of the disaster areas. This acoustic imaging innovation utilizes sound waves to make high-goal pictures of the ocean bottom, uncovering lowered highlights with astounding clearness. The Victoria Waterway Undertaking conveyed side-check sonar to overview the hunt region, covering far reaching areas of the seabed in a purposeful and careful way efficiently. The subsequent pictures gave a definite perspective on the submerged geography, empowering specialists to distinguish oddities and potential wreck locales.

When potential locales were distinguished through side-examine sonar, ROVs and AUVs were conveyed for itemized investigations. These remotely worked and independent vehicles permitted scientists to investigate the submerged climate progressively, catching superior quality video film and pictures. The capacity to remotely explore and move these vehicles at profundities inaccessible by jumpers demonstrated essential in the quest for the Franklin Undertaking wrecks.

The submerged investigation of HMS Erebus and HMS Fear uncovered strikingly very much safeguarded conditions, offering an intriguing look into the past. The cold and dull waters of the Icy gave a climate helpful for the protection of natural materials, including wood, materials, and, surprisingly, a portion of the team's very own effects. The disaster areas became time containers, frozen in a crossroads ever, and their revelation brought up new issues about the occasions prompting the campaign's lamentable end.

The discoveries from the disaster areas tested existing stories and added to a more nuanced comprehension of the Franklin Campaign. The ancient rarities recuperated, including navigational instruments, individual things, and arrangements, gave substantial connections to the day to day routines of the team. The all around protected condition of the disaster areas additionally offered signs about the circumstances looked by the group, revealing insight into perspectives, for example, lead harming from ineffectively safeguarded canned products.

The mechanical headways in marine prehistoric studies not just worked with the disclosure of the Franklin Endeavor wrecks yet additionally opened new wildernesses in the investigation of submerged legacy. The utilization of cutting edge imaging methods, for example, photogrammetry and 3D displaying, permitted analysts to make definite and precise portrayals of the disaster areas and their general surroundings. These advanced recreations serve as significant devices for documentation as well as vivid instructive assets for general society.

The protection of submerged legacy presents special difficulties, and the disclosure of very much safeguarded wrecks like those of the Franklin Campaign gives significant experiences into preservation techniques. The outrageous states of the Icy, with its cool temperatures and low oxygen levels, added to the astounding condition of conservation. Nonetheless, the disaster areas are not invulnerable to natural dangers, and continuous checking and preservation endeavors are crucial for protect these verifiable antiques.

The revelation of HMS Erebus and HMS Dread additionally highlighted the interdisciplinary idea of marine paleontology. Analysts from different fields, including paleohistory, history, sea life science, and ecological science, teamed up to unwind the insider facts of the disaster areas. The joining of logical mastery, mechanical development, and verifiable request embodies the all encompassing methodology expected for thorough submerged investigation.

Past the archeological importance, the disclosure of the Franklin Campaign wrecks touched off a reestablished interest in Cold investigation and sea history. The disaster areas became central focuses for research, public commitment, and worldwide coordinated effort. The documentation and investigation of the disaster areas contribute not exclusively to how we might interpret the Franklin Endeavor yet in addition to more extensive conversations about the effect of environmental change on the Icy district and the moral contemplations of submerged investigation.

The mechanical headways that assumed a urgent part in the disclosure of HMS Erebus and HMS Fear likewise feature the developing idea of marine paleontology as a field. As new innovations keep on arising, from cutting edge sensors to man-made reasoning applications, the opportunities for revealing and archiving submerged legacy grow. These innovative devices upgrade the proficiency of investigation as well as empower analysts to dig further into the intricacies of verifiable stories lowered underneath the waves.

The revelation of the Franklin Campaign wrecks addresses a victory of human inventiveness, tirelessness, and cooperation. It is a demonstration of the persevering quest for information and the utilization of state of the art innovation to settle verifiable secrets. The disaster areas, when lost in the boundlessness of the Icy, presently act as unmistakable connections to the past, offering a brief look into the difficulties looked by the team and the untold accounts of the disastrous endeavor.

The disclosure of HMS Erebus and HMS Fear and the ensuing progressions in marine prehistoric studies have not just disentangled the secrets of the disastrous Franklin Endeavor yet additionally re-imagined the conceivable outcomes and procedures inside the field of submerged investigation. The victory of finding the surprisingly safeguarded wrecks in the freezing waters of the Cold addresses a demonstration of human flexibility, mechanical development, and the voracious mission for information.

This part dives further into the diverse ramifications of this revelation, going from its effect on authentic stories to its importance in the more extensive setting of ecological changes and moral contemplations.

The very much safeguarded condition of the disaster areas, typified neglected and dull profundities of the Cold seabed, has given a phenomenal chance to rework the authentic story of the Franklin Campaign. Ancient rarities recuperated from the disaster areas, going from navigational instruments to individual effects of the team, have offered unmistakable connections to the past. These things, frozen in time for almost two centuries, give experiences into the regular routines, difficulties, and goals of the people who left on this hazardous excursion. The relics contribute not exclusively to the particular story of the Franklin Endeavor yet additionally to a more extensive comprehension of nineteenth century oceanic investigation and the intricacies of life in the Icy.

The mechanical developments that assumed a focal part in the revelation and ensuing investigation of the disaster areas have fundamentally progressed the field of marine prehistoric studies. The utilization of side-examine sonar, remotely worked vehicles (ROVs), and independent submerged vehicles (AUVs) epitomizes the incorporation of state of the art innovation into the investigation of submerged legacy. These devices have worked with the disclosure of the disaster areas as well as permitted analysts to record, investigate, and protect the locales with remarkable accuracy.

Side-check sonar, specifically, has been instrumental in reviewing huge region of the Cold seabed with striking subtlety. The acoustic imaging innovation utilized in side-filter sonar makes high-goal pictures that give an extensive outline of the submerged scene. The deliberate studying of the hunt region, directed by side-check sonar, empowered analysts to recognize peculiarities and potential wreck destinations, eventually prompting the disclosure of HMS Erebus and HMS Fear.

The organization of ROVs and AUVs added one more layer of refinement to the investigation interaction. These remotely worked and independent vehicles permitted specialists to explore the difficult submerged climate progressively. Outfitted with superior quality cameras, these vehicles caught nitty gritty symbolism and film of the disaster areas, adding to a more nuanced comprehension of their circumstances. The capacity to investigate profundities past the span of human jumpers has been a distinct advantage, permitting specialists to explore and record the destinations with unrivaled accuracy.

The headways in marine archaic exploration stretch out past the simple revelation of wrecks; they have worked with the production of vivid advanced portrayals of the submerged locales. Methods, for example, photogrammetry and 3D demonstrating have been utilized to create definite recreations of the disaster areas and their general surroundings. These advanced models act as important devices for documentation, investigation, and instructive effort.

They not just give scientists exhaustive datasets for additional concentrate yet in addition offer the public a valuable chance to draw in with the verifiable curios in a virtual space.

The safeguarding of submerged legacy, exemplified by the very much saved wrecks of the Franklin Endeavor, is a sensitive harmony among investigation and protection. The outrageous states of the Icy, portrayed by chilly temperatures and low oxygen levels, have added to the outstanding condition of conservation. Be that as it may, the disaster areas are not invulnerable to ecological dangers, and the effect of environmental change on the Icy district raises worries about the drawn out soundness of these submerged locales.

The revelations of HMS Erebus and HMS Dread have touched off a reestablished interest in Icy investigation and sea history on a worldwide scale. The disaster areas have become central focuses for global cooperation, research drives, and public commitment. The accounts rising up out of the disaster areas rise above public limits, inciting cooperative endeavors to study, protect, and share the verifiable meaning of these submerged locales.

The interdisciplinary idea of the examination encompassing the Franklin Endeavor wrecks mirrors the all encompassing methodology expected for extensive submerged investigation. Coordinated effort between archeologists, history specialists, sea life scholars, ecological researchers, and specialists from different fields has improved the comprehension of the disaster areas and their context oriented importance. This cooperative exertion highlights the interconnectedness of various disciplines in disentangling the intricacies of authentic accounts lowered underneath the waves.

Notwithstanding the logical and verifiable perspectives, the revelation of the disaster areas raises moral contemplations with respect to submerged investigation and the protection of social legacy. The disaster areas of HMS Erebus and HMS Dread are not only ancient rarities yet additionally act as gravesites for the team individuals who died during the Franklin Undertaking. The requirement for aware and moral investigation rehearses is fundamental, adjusting the quest for information with the protection of the pride and memory of the people who lost their lives.

The effective disclosure of the Franklin Endeavor wrecks addresses a change in perspective in the potential outcomes of submerged investigation. As innovation keeps on progressing, from additional refined sensors to man-made reasoning applications, the fate of marine paleohistory holds invigorating potential. The continuous investigation of submerged legacy contributes not exclusively to verifiable stories yet additionally to contemporary conversations on ecological manageability, moral investigation, and the obligations related with revealing the mysteries of the profound.

The disclosure of HMS Erebus and HMS Fear and the mechanical headways in marine prehistoric studies comprise an extraordinary section in the investigation of submerged legacy. The very much safeguarded wrecks, uncovered through the combination of state of the art innovation and interdisciplinary cooperation, have reshaped how we might interpret the Franklin Undertaking and nineteenth century Icy investigation. The ramifications of this revelation reach out past the domains of history and paleohistory, addressing ecological changes, mechanical advancement, and moral contemplations in the field of submerged investigation. The disaster areas of the Franklin Endeavor, when lost in the frozen hug of the Icy, presently stand as piercing images of human resourcefulness, flexibility, and the persevering through mission to open the secrets of the past.

Chapter 3

The Bermuda Triangle
Fact or Fiction?

The Bermuda Triangle, a district in the western piece of the North Atlantic Sea, has for some time been covered in secret and hypothesis, spellbinding the minds of individuals all over the planet. Frequently alluded to as "Satan's Triangle," this region is famous for supposed vanishings of boats and airplane under secretive conditions. The mystery of the Bermuda Triangle has powered various hypotheses, going from regular clarifications to extraterrestrial peculiarities, however the inquiry perseveres: is the Bermuda Triangle a genuine risk zone or just a result of legend and deception?

Verifiable Viewpoint:

The legend of the Bermuda Triangle acquired noticeable quality during the twentieth hundred years, with a progression of high-profile episodes and sensationalized reports catching public consideration. One of the earliest episodes frequently connected to the Bermuda Triangle is the vanishing of Flight 19 in December 1945.

This unit of five U.S. Naval force aircraft evaporated during a normal preparation mission, prompting a hunt and salvage mission that likewise brought about the vanishing of a salvage plane. The secretive conditions encompassing Flight 19 powered hypothesis and set up for the Bermuda Triangle legend.

In the many years that followed, different episodes, including the vanishing of the big hauler SS Marine Sulfur Sovereign in 1963 and the evaporating of a freight transport named SS El Faro in 2015, have been credited to the Bermuda Triangle. Notwithstanding, basic examination uncovers that large numbers of these episodes have conceivable clarifications established in regular peculiarities, human blunder, or specialized disappointments.

Geological Limits:

The Bermuda Triangle is approximately characterized, with various sources giving changing limits. For the most part, it is accepted to include the places of Miami (Florida, USA), Bermuda, and San Juan (Puerto Rico). This three-sided region covers a huge part of the western North Atlantic, known for its weighty oceanic and air traffic. While certain defenders of the Bermuda Triangle fantasy grow its limits to incorporate the Azores and the Waterways of Florida, others contend that the occurrences credited to the area are genuinely immaterial while considering the volume of traffic going through it.

Normal Peculiarities and Natural Elements:

Logical examinations concerning the Bermuda Triangle have reliably exposed extraordinary or extraterrestrial clarifications. All things being equal, scientists highlight various normal peculiarities and natural factors that can add to oceanic and flight episodes in the area.

One such element is the Inlet Stream, a strong sea momentum that moves through the Bermuda Triangle. The Bay Stream can make violent and capricious ocean conditions, possibly causing navigational difficulties for ships. Furthermore, the locale is inclined to abrupt and serious weather conditions changes, including extreme tempests and waterspouts. These climate peculiarities can present critical perils to sea and aeronautical route.

Methane Hydrates:

A few speculations recommend that the Bermuda Triangle's seabed might contain enormous stores of methane hydrates, a translucent type of methane caught in ice. As per these speculations, abrupt arrivals of methane gas from the sea floor could diminish the water's thickness, making shakiness and compromising lightness for ships. In any case, logical agreement doesn't uphold the possibility that methane hydrates assume a huge part in the Bermuda Triangle's supposed vanishings. The presence of enormous methane hydrate stores isn't remarkable to this district, and the circumstances expected for an unexpected delivery are far-fetched.

Human Blunder and Specialized Disappointments:

Numerous occurrences ascribed to the Bermuda Triangle can be followed back to human blunder or specialized disappointments. Pilots or guides new to the area's difficult circumstances might commit errors, prompting mishaps. Mechanical disappointments in airplane or vessels, intensified by unfavorable atmospheric conditions, can add to occurrences without summoning powerful clarifications.

Absence of Measurable Importance:

Factual examinations of occurrences in the Bermuda Triangle uncover that the recurrence of mishaps in this space isn't lopsided to other vigorously dealt districts. Specialists contend that the Bermuda Triangle fantasy has been propagated by specific announcing, drama, and the exclusion of significant subtleties in certain records. While considering the huge number of boats and planes that navigate the locale routinely, the purportedly baffling vanishings become genuinely irrelevant.

Search and Salvage Activities:

Pundits of the Bermuda Triangle legend bring up that, in opposition to its standing as a peril zone, the locale is home to broad hunt and salvage tasks led by the US Coast Gatekeeper and other global organizations. The presence of deep rooted salvage endeavors shows a commonsense affirmation of the district's difficulties instead of an acknowledgment of heavenly or incomprehensible occasions.

Incredulous Viewpoints:

Doubters contend that the Bermuda Triangle fantasy is a blend of drama, metropolitan legends, and a distortion of information. They battle that the clear bunch of episodes in the area can be made sense of by the union of numerous variables, including human blunder, antagonistic weather patterns, and mechanical disappointments. The specific accentuation on strange vanishings, while disregarding occurrences with clear clarifications, adds to the fantasy's propagation.

Media Melodrama:

The media plays had a huge impact in enhancing the secrets of the Bermuda Triangle, frequently focusing on shocking stories over genuine revealing. Books, narratives, and articles have propagated the legend, introducing speculative hypotheses without thorough logical investigation. The appeal of the unexplained and the paranormal has added to the getting through prominence of the Bermuda Triangle in mainstream society.

in any case, they fall inside the domain of known and grasped factors. The persona encompassing the Bermuda Triangle has continued because of a blend of verifiable occurrences, media melodrama, and the human tendency towards the baffling and unexplained.

One viewpoint frequently disregarded in conversations about the Bermuda Triangle is the limitlessness of the locale and the high volume of oceanic and airborne traffic it encounters. The triangle envelops one of the most active delivery paths on the planet, interfacing significant ports and working with worldwide exchange. The sheer extent of vessels traveling the region improves the probability of mishaps, specialized disappointments, or human blunders happening, as would be normal in any vigorously dealt district.

The Bermuda Triangle fantasy acquired conspicuousness during the twentieth 100 years, filled by emotional accounts encompassing vanishings and affirmed paranormal occasions. The episode including Flight 19, a group of U.S. Naval force planes, in 1945 is much of the time refered to as a foundation of the Bermuda Triangle legend. Nonetheless, closer assessment uncovers that Flight 19 probably succumbed to a mix of navigational blunders, fuel weariness, and testing weather patterns. The vanishing of a salvage plane during the ensuing inquiry mission can be credited to comparable variables.

Essentially, the instance of the SS Marine Sulfur Sovereign, a big hauler that evaporated in 1963, has been dependent upon speculative hypotheses connecting it to the Bermuda Triangle. In any case, a more careful examination revealed proof proposing that the vessel was ineffectively kept up with and reasonable capitulated to primary disappointment during unfriendly weather patterns. The conditions encompassing the SS El Faro, a freight transport that sank in 2015, likewise embody the difficulties presented by the capricious climate in the locale. The vessel experienced a strong storm, and its lamentable destiny was an outcome of both ecological elements and direction.

Meteorological peculiarities, like waterspouts, have been proposed as expected supporters of the Bermuda Triangle legend. Waterspouts, twisters that structure over water, can represent a danger to boats and airplane. Nonetheless, their event isn't select to the Bermuda Triangle, and they are experienced in different regions of the planet. The unexpected and erratic nature of waterspouts might have added to the view of the Bermuda Triangle as a risky region.

Besides, headways in innovation and navigational guides have fundamentally upgraded the wellbeing of oceanic and aeronautical travel. Present day vessels and airplane are outfitted with modern correspondence frameworks, weather conditions estimating apparatuses, and route instruments that relieve the dangers related with testing conditions. The encounters of the past, when route depended all the more vigorously on simple instruments and manual computations, are less appropriate in the contemporary setting.

Perceiving the effect of media melodrama on the propagation of the Bermuda Triangle myth is critical. Emotional accounts of puzzling vanishings and unexplained peculiarities catch public premium and creative mind, adding to the legend's getting through claim. Books, narratives, and fictitious depictions frequently underscore the electrifying parts of the Bermuda Triangle while making light of or excluding normal clarifications for occurrences.

Rather than the electrifying accounts, logical examinations and extensive investigations of the Bermuda Triangle have reliably neglected to distinguish any examples or irregularities that warrant extraordinary clarifications. The factual examination of episodes in the district exhibits that the event of mishaps is steady with worldwide midpoints for vigorously dealt regions. The shortfall of any logically approved proof supporting paranormal or extraterrestrial inclusion highlights the speculative idea of the Bermuda Triangle legend.

The utilization of Occam's razor, a rule pushing for the least complex clarification when confronted with contending speculations, is important in assessing the Bermuda Triangle peculiarity. The most direct and deductively upheld clarifications for episodes in the area include referred to elements like atmospheric conditions, navigational difficulties, human mistake, and specialized disappointments. Incidental hypotheses summoning outsider kidnappings, time travels, or submerged oddities need experimental help and are pointless to make sense of the noticed peculiarities.

The Bermuda Triangle fantasy has endured because of its entrenchment in mainstream society, where it fills in as an enthralling account for narrating, books, motion pictures, and TV. The charm of the unexplained and the puzzling keeps on catching public interest, prompting a propagation of the legend notwithstanding the absence of observational proof. It is fundamental for approach conversations about the Bermuda Triangle with a basic focal point, recognizing the verifiable occurrences inside the setting of known factors and scattering the persona that has encircled the locale for a really long time.

The Bermuda Triangle stays a persevering through mystery that has caught the public's creative mind for quite a long time. Notwithstanding, a complete examination of the accessible proof, logical examinations, and verifiable episodes uncovers that the legend needs exact help. The implied secrets of the Bermuda Triangle can be credited to a mix of regular peculiarities, human blunder, and media sentimentality. While the locale might present navigational difficulties because of its weather patterns and weighty traffic, there is no logical reason for ascribing baffling vanishings to paranormal or extraterrestrial variables. As how we might interpret the world and mechanical capacities keep on propelling, moving toward conversations about the Bermuda Triangle with a sane and basic viewpoint, isolating reality from fiction in the mission for truth is fundamental.

3.1 Introduction to the legendary Bermuda Triangle and its reputation for mysterious disappearances.

The Bermuda Triangle, a locale settled in the western piece of the North Atlantic Sea, has developed an unbelievable standing as a secretive and dangerous region where boats and airplane apparently disappear suddenly.

Frequently alluded to as "Satan's Triangle," this puzzling stretch of sea has caught the minds of individuals around the world, becoming inseparable from unexplained peculiarities and otherworldly events. In this investigation, we set out on an excursion into the core of the Bermuda Triangle, diving into its verifiable setting, the tales that have sustained its persona, and the logical examination pointed toward disentangling reality behind its standing.

The geological limits of the Bermuda Triangle are enigmatically characterized, commonly including a region between the marks of Miami (Florida, USA), Bermuda, and San Juan (Puerto Rico). This three-sided region has acquired reputation for its relationship with a progression of purportedly puzzling vanishings of boats and airplane. The legends encompassing the Bermuda Triangle have become profoundly imbued in mainstream society, sustained by books, narratives, and sensationalized media inclusion.

Perhaps of the earliest episode that added to the legend of the Bermuda Triangle happened in December 1945, with the baffling vanishing of Flight 19. This unit of five U.S. Naval force aircraft evaporated during a standard preparation mission, setting off a pursuit and salvage mission that, shockingly, likewise brought about the vanishing of a salvage plane. The conditions encompassing Flight 19 filled hypothesis and laid the basis for the Bermuda Triangle fantasy. Resulting occurrences, for example, the disappearing of the big hauler SS Marine Sulfur Sovereign in 1963 and the sinking of the freight transport SS El Faro in 2015, have additionally energized the persona of the area.

While the Bermuda Triangle has become inseparable from stories of baffling vanishings, it is fundamental to investigate the authentic setting and accounts that have added to its amazing status. The district is known for its weighty sea and air traffic, filling in as a vital junction for delivery paths and flight ways. The union of significant ports, worldwide shipping lanes, and occupied air hallways makes it a center for transportation, definitely prompting a higher volume of occurrences. As we explore through the fascinating history of the Bermuda Triangle, it becomes basic to recognize authentic events, speculative stories, and the persevering through appeal of the unexplained.

The appeal of the Bermuda Triangle is well established in the narratives of disappeared boats and airplane, frequently joined by shocking subtleties and mysterious conditions. In any case, a nearer assessment of these occurrences uncovers a more nuanced picture, where regular peculiarities, human mistake, and specialized disappointments might give normal clarifications. The vanishing of Flight 19, for instance, is currently accepted to be a consequence of navigational blunders, fuel fatigue, and testing weather patterns instead of powerful powers. The resulting vanishing of the salvage plane during the inquiry mission can be ascribed to comparable variables.

The SS Marine Sulfur Sovereign, a big hauler that evaporated in 1963, has been related with the Bermuda Triangle legend, yet a careful examination recommended that the vessel probably surrendered to primary disappointment during unfriendly weather patterns. The heartbreaking sinking of the SS El Faro in 2015 happened amidst a strong tropical storm, highlighting the district's helplessness to flighty climate peculiarities. These episodes, when seen from the perspective of known factors, give an additional grounded point of view on the implied secrets of the Bermuda Triangle.

The topographical highlights of the Bermuda Triangle, including the strong sea ebb and flow known as the Bay Stream, have been embroiled in the district's reputation. The Bay Stream, a quick and warm sea momentum, moves through the Bermuda Triangle and can make violent and eccentric ocean conditions. Also, the locale is inclined to unexpected and extraordinary weather conditions changes, including serious tempests and waterspouts. While these normal peculiarities present difficulties to oceanic and ethereal route, they fall inside the domain of known and figured out factors.

Speculative hypotheses have likewise been proposed to make sense of the Bermuda Triangle's unbelievable status, including the presence of methane hydrates on the sea depths. Some recommend that abrupt arrivals of methane gas from the seabed could lessen the water's thickness, making insecurity and compromising the lightness of boats. In any case, the logical agreement doesn't uphold the possibility that methane hydrates assume a huge part in the Bermuda Triangle's supposed vanishings. The presence of enormous methane hydrate stores isn't interesting to this district, and the circumstances expected for an unexpected delivery are far-fetched.

The charm of the unexplained and the strange has frequently eclipsed judicious clarifications for episodes inside the Bermuda Triangle. The media, specifically, plays had a huge impact in enhancing the locale's persona, sensationalizing accounts of vanishings and adding to the propagation of the fantasy. Books, narratives, and fictitious depictions have additionally dug in the Bermuda Triangle in mainstream society as a domain where reality obscures with the powerful.

Logical examinations concerning the Bermuda Triangle have reliably exposed extraordinary or extraterrestrial clarifications. All things considered, specialists highlight different normal peculiarities and natural factors that can add to sea and avionics episodes in the locale. Side-check sonar, an innovation that utilizations sound waves to make high-goal pictures of the ocean bottom, plays had a critical impact in reviewing the Bermuda Triangle's submerged scene. Remotely worked vehicles (ROVs) and independent submerged vehicles (AUVs) have been sent for point by point reviews, catching superior quality video film and pictures.

The submerged investigation of the Bermuda Triangle has uncovered surprisingly very much saved conditions in certain region, offering an uncommon look into the past. The cold and dim waters of the Atlantic Sea give a climate helpful for the protection of natural materials, including wood, materials, and, surprisingly, a portion of the group's very own effects. The disaster areas inside the Bermuda Triangle have become time containers, frozen in a crossroads ever, and their investigation brings up new issues about the occasions prompting their death.

The mechanical headways in marine antiquarianism not just work with the investigation of submerged destinations inside the Bermuda Triangle yet in addition open new outskirts in the comprehension of lowered verifiable stories. The utilization of cutting edge imaging strategies, for example, photogrammetry and 3D displaying, permits specialists to make point by point and exact portrayals of wrecks and their general surroundings. These computerized reproductions serve as important apparatuses for documentation as well as vivid instructive assets for the general population.

The protection of submerged legacy inside the Bermuda Triangle presents remarkable difficulties, and continuous checking and preservation endeavors are crucial for shield these authentic antiques. The disaster areas, with their rich stores of data, contribute not exclusively to the comprehension of explicit occurrences yet in addition to more extensive conversations about sea history, route, and the difficulties of investigation in the untamed ocean.

The Bermuda Triangle fantasy has endured because of a blend of verifiable episodes, media sentimentality, and the human interest with the unexplored world.

The area's infamous standing keeps on spellbinding people in general, causing to notice accounts of evaporated boats and airplane. In any case, a basic assessment of the accessible proof uncovers that the Bermuda Triangle's secrets can be credited to a combination of regular peculiarities, navigational difficulties, and the notions of the vast ocean.

As we explore the complicated accounts and logical examinations encompassing the Bermuda Triangle, it becomes apparent that the unbelievable status of this district is profoundly laced with the human longing for secret and the other-worldly. The Bermuda Triangle, with its stories of puzzling vanishings and strange profundities, stays an image of the cryptic and the neglected. In the accompanying segments, we will dig further into the logical points of view, verifiable setting, and progressing investigations that shape how we might interpret the Bermuda Triangle.

The Bermuda Triangle, frequently named "Satan's Triangle," keeps on remaining as an image of secret and interest, dazzling the human creative mind with its standing for puzzling vanishings. As we dig further into the domain of this incredible region, it's essential to investigate the logical viewpoints that challenge the persona encompassing the Bermuda Triangle. By looking at regular peculiarities, mechanical progressions, and measurable investigations, we can unwind the intricacies of this mystery and separate reality from fiction.

One of the predominant logical clarifications for occurrences inside the Bermuda Triangle lies in the assembly of normal peculiarities. The Inlet Stream, a strong sea momentum moving through the locale, is known for making tempestuous and eccentric ocean conditions. The quick waters of the Bay Stream can present difficulties to route, particularly for vessels experiencing unfriendly weather patterns. This regular power, while not elite to the Bermuda Triangle, adds to the district's reputation as a difficult and possibly unsafe region for sea travel.

Meteorological peculiarities, like waterspouts, have additionally been embroiled in the Bermuda Triangle legend. Waterspouts, cyclones that structure over water, can represent a danger to boats and airplane. These alternating sections of air, while entrancing and possibly perilous, are not remarkable to the Bermuda Triangle and can happen in different regions of the planet. The unexpected and flighty nature of waterspouts might have added to the view of the Bermuda Triangle as a dangerous region, further energizing its persona.

Mechanical progressions in marine prehistoric studies play had a urgent impact in investigating the submerged scene of the Bermuda Triangle. Side-examine sonar, an innovation that utilizations sound waves to make point by point pictures of the ocean bottom, has been instrumental in reviewing immense region of the sea. This acoustic imaging method permits scientists to distinguish submerged highlights and irregularities, supporting the quest for wrecks and curios. The utilization of side-filter sonar has given significant experiences into the submerged geography of the

Bermuda Triangle, assisting specialists with understanding the circumstances that might add to occurrences in the district.

Notwithstanding side-check sonar, remotely worked vehicles (ROVs) and independent submerged vehicles (AUVs) have been sent to investigate the disaster areas inside the Bermuda Triangle. These cutting edge innovations permit scientists to lead nitty gritty assessments of submerged locales, catching superior quality video film and pictures. The capacity to remotely explore and move these vehicles at profundities inaccessible by human jumpers is essential for investigating the difficult submerged climate of the Bermuda Triangle. The bits of knowledge acquired from these mechanical devices add to a more thorough comprehension of the disaster areas and their verifiable importance.

The disaster areas inside the Bermuda Triangle, strikingly very much protected neglected and dim waters of the Atlantic Sea, offer a one of a kind look into the past. Relics recuperated from these disaster areas, going from navigational instruments to individual effects of the group, give substantial connections to the authentic stories of sea investigation. The safeguarding of natural materials, for example, wood and materials, inside the disaster areas has made time containers that offer a window into the circumstances looked by the individuals who cruised through the Bermuda Triangle.

The utilization of cutting edge imaging procedures, including photogrammetry and 3D displaying, has additionally upgraded the investigation and documentation of wrecks inside the Bermuda Triangle. These innovations permit scientists to make point by point and exact portrayals of the submerged locales, creating three-layered models of wrecks and their general surroundings. The advanced reproductions act as significant apparatuses for investigation, documentation, and instructive effort. They not just add to the logical comprehension of the disaster areas yet in addition give vivid encounters to people in general, encouraging an association with the verifiable curios.

While the Bermuda Triangle has acquired reputation for its relationship with strange vanishings, factual investigations uncover a more nuanced point of view. The recurrence of mishaps inside the Bermuda Triangle, when contrasted with other vigorously dealt districts, doesn't display an unbalanced example. Pundits contend that the fantasy has been propagated by specific revealing, media drama, and the oversight of vital subtleties in certain records. While considering the huge number of boats and planes that cross the area routinely, the purportedly strange vanishings become genuinely immaterial.

Search and salvage activities inside the Bermuda Triangle are broad, including the US Coast Watchman and global organizations. The area is outfitted with deeply grounded conventions for answering misery calls and occurrences. The presence of powerful hunt and salvage endeavors goes against the idea of the Bermuda Triangle as an intrinsically hazardous or secretive region. All things considered, it mirrors a logical affirmation of the difficulties presented by the locale's weather patterns, navigational intricacies, and weighty traffic.

As we explore the logical viewpoints encompassing the Bermuda Triangle, it becomes obvious that the unbelievable status of this district is an intricate transaction of normal powers, verifiable occurrences, and human interest with the unexplored world. While the Bermuda Triangle keeps on catching public creative mind as a domain of strange vanishings, the logical examination applied to its peculiarities disentangles the layers of fantasy and deception.

The verifiable setting of the Bermuda Triangle, with its relationship with Flight 19, the SS Marine Sulfur Sovereign, and the SS El Faro, mirrors an intermingling of navigational difficulties, unfriendly weather patterns, and human mistake. Investigating these occurrences inside the structure of realized factors gives a normal and grounded comprehension of the occasions that have added to the Bermuda Triangle's persona.

The Bermuda Triangle stays an incredible and cryptic region, characterized by its standing for puzzling vanishings and unexplained peculiarities. Logical viewpoints, established in the investigation of normal powers, mechanical progressions, and factual examinations, give a nuanced comprehension of the locale. The combination of the Inlet Stream, meteorological peculiarities, and the utilization of cutting edge imaging advancements has demystified a few parts of the Bermuda Triangle.

While the appeal of the unexplained endures, the logical examination applied to verifiable occurrences challenges the extraordinary stories encompassing this unbelievable region. The Bermuda Triangle, with its stories of disappeared boats and airplane, keeps on enticing pioneers, specialists, and lovers into its profundities, welcoming a sensitive harmony among fantasy and reality in the mission for understanding.

3.2 Scientific investigations into the true nature of the region's hazards.

Logical examinations concerning the real essence of the risks inside the Bermuda Triangle have been instrumental in demystifying the amazing standing related with this baffling district. While the Bermuda Triangle has for some time been inseparable from puzzling vanishings, a nearer assessment from the perspective of logical request uncovers a more nuanced and reasonable comprehension of the difficulties looked by those exploring its waters and airspace.

One of the key normal variables adding to the district's difficulties is the Inlet Stream, a strong sea momentum moving through the Bermuda Triangle. The Bay Stream, starting in the Bay of Mexico, streams along the eastern shore of the US prior to arriving at the North Atlantic. This quick and warm flow can make violent and eccentric ocean conditions, presenting navigational difficulties for vessels traveling the region. While the Bay Stream is an irrefutable and perceived maritime peculiarity, its effect on the Bermuda Triangle's oceanic exercises has been huge.

The quick waters of the Inlet Stream can prompt the formation of testing waves and ocean conditions, particularly while cooperating with restricting breezes or unfavorable climate. Sailors exploring through this locale might experience difficult situations and strong flows, requiring talented seamanship and exact route. Nonetheless, these difficulties are important for the normal elements of the sea and don't include secretive or unexplained powers. Logical examinations have zeroed in on understanding the way of behaving of the Bay Stream and its impact on the oceanic exercises inside the Bermuda Triangle, giving significant bits of knowledge to safe route.

Meteorological peculiarities, like serious tempests, tropical storms, and waterspouts, further add to the perils looked by boats and airplane in the Bermuda Triangle. The district is known for its helplessness to unexpected and extreme weather conditions changes, a trademark credited to its area in the western piece of the North Atlantic. The assembly of warm and cold air masses, joined with the presence of the Inlet Stream, establishes a climate helpful for the development of strong tempests.

Tropical storms, specifically, are a typical event in the Atlantic bowl, and the Bermuda Triangle isn't excluded from their effect. These typhoons can areas of strength for bring, weighty precipitation, and difficult situations, making dangerous circumstances for sea and elevated exercises.

The authentic episodes related with the Bermuda Triangle frequently concur with the event of serious climate occasions, featuring the job of normal powers in forming the locale's difficulties.

Waterspouts, cyclones that structure over water, address one more meteorological peculiarity experienced inside the Bermuda Triangle. While waterspouts can be outwardly striking and possibly risky, their event isn't elite to this area. Waterspouts are seen in different regions of the planet and are a result of explicit climatic circumstances, remembering the presence of warm water and flimsiness for the air.

Logical examinations concerning the meteorological parts of the Bermuda Triangle have zeroed in on grasping the examples of weather conditions changes and distinguishing the variables adding to the development of tempests and waterspouts. Meteorologists use progressed estimating strategies, satellite symbolism, and weather conditions models to give precise and convenient data to sailors and pilots exploring through the area. By acquiring an exhaustive comprehension of the meteorological circumstances inside the Bermuda Triangle, researchers add to upgraded wellbeing measures and hazard relief for those crossing its waters and airspace.

Mechanical headways in route and correspondence play had a significant impact in moderating the perils related with the Bermuda Triangle. Current vessels and airplane are furnished with complex route frameworks, radar, and specialized gadgets that give continuous data about atmospheric conditions, navigational risks, and other important information. The reconciliation of Worldwide Situating Framework (GPS) innovation has upset route, permitting exact assurance of a vessel's or alternately airplane's area, speed, and heading.

The accessibility of precise and solid navigational guides altogether decreases the gamble of occurrences connected with navigational blunders inside the Bermuda Triangle. Sailors and pilots can get convenient updates on weather conditions changes, possible perils, and ideal courses, empowering them to pursue informed choices and explore securely through the district. The execution of cutting edge correspondence frameworks further works with quick reaction to crises and upgrades coordination in search and salvage activities.

The factual examination of episodes inside the Bermuda Triangle is one more part of logical examination pointed toward dispersing the fantasy of secretive vanishings. Pundits contend that the district's reputation is excessively swelled because of specific announcing, media drama, and the exclusion of critical subtleties in certain records. By analyzing the recurrence of mishaps in the Bermuda Triangle in contrast with other vigorously dealt locales, specialists have looked to contextualize the implied secrets.

Factual investigations have uncovered that the Bermuda Triangle doesn't display an uncommonly high pace of mishaps when standardized for the volume of oceanic and ethereal traffic it encounters.

The locale fills in as a basic junction for delivery paths and flight ways, bringing about a higher volume of vessels and airplane navigating its waters and airspace. While considering the sheer number of oceanic and aeronautical exercises, the announced episodes inside the Bermuda Triangle line up with worldwide midpoints for vigorously dealt regions.

Search and salvage activities inside the Bermuda Triangle, facilitated by the US Coast Watchman and global organizations, highlight the locale's obligation to somewhere safe and crisis reaction. The presence of deep rooted search and salvage conventions goes against the thought of the Bermuda Triangle as an intrinsically hazardous or secretive region. All things considered, it mirrors an even minded way to deal with tending to the difficulties presented by unfavorable weather patterns, navigational intricacies, and the high volume of traffic.

While logical examinations have demystified numerous parts of the perils inside the Bermuda Triangle, the locale keeps on being a point of convergence for continuous examination and investigation. The safeguarding of submerged legacy, including the disaster areas of boats that met their destiny in the Bermuda Triangle, gives a one of a kind chance to reveal verifiable stories and gain experiences into past oceanic exercises. The utilization of cutting edge imaging advancements, like side-filter sonar and remotely worked vehicles, permits scientists to investigate the submerged scene and archive the states of wrecks with extraordinary detail.

As mainstream researchers keeps on unwinding the intricacies of the Bermuda Triangle, it becomes obvious that the perils looked by sailors and pilots are established in normal powers, navigational difficulties, and unfavorable weather patterns. The incorporation of logical information, mechanical progressions, and measurable investigations adds to a far reaching comprehension of the district's elements. By scattering the legend of strange vanishings and zeroing in on proof based clarifications, researchers make ready for a more precise and normal view of the Bermuda Triangle.

The continuous investigation and logical examination of the Bermuda Triangle have dispersed the fantasy of strange vanishings as well as opened new roads for grasping the district's exceptional geographical and maritime attributes. The geographical elements of the ocean bottom inside the Bermuda Triangle have been a subject of interest, with specialists looking to unwind the submerged scene and its likely impact on sea exercises.

Bathymetric examinations, which include planning the ocean bottom geography, have given significant experiences into the shapes and geographical arrangements underneath the Bermuda Triangle. The utilization of cutting edge sonar innovation has permitted researchers to make nitty gritty guides that feature submerged highlights like edges, channels, and lowered structures. This planning has added to a superior comprehension of the difficulties looked by vessels exploring through the district.

One striking geographical component is the presence of remote ocean channels, including the Puerto Rico Channel, which is the most profound piece of the Atlantic Sea. The Puerto Rico Channel, situated toward the north of the Caribbean Ocean, is known for its outrageous profundity, arriving at profundities surpassing 8,300 meters (27,230 feet). While remote ocean channels are not select to the Bermuda Triangle, their presence adds a layer of intricacy to the district's submerged geology.

The communication between remote ocean channels, submerged flows, and geographical designs can impact the way of behaving of maritime waters inside the Bermuda Triangle. Analysts have investigated the elements of these cooperations to comprehend how they might add to the area's navigational difficulties. While the remote ocean channels themselves are not intrinsically unsafe to vessels, their presence can impact the development of sea flows and possibly make conditions that require cautious route.

The Bermuda Triangle's standing for puzzling vanishings has additionally been connected to the peculiarity of rebel waves. Rebel waves are incredibly huge and startling maritime waves that can represent a critical danger to vessels. While once thought to be a marine legend, the event of maverick waves has been reported through satellite symbolism and logical perceptions. These waves, which can arrive at levels of 25 meters (82 feet) or more, are many times the aftereffect of the union of various wave frameworks and can get sailors unsuspecting.

The remarkable blend of submerged geography, sea flows, and weather conditions inside the Bermuda Triangle might add to the development of rebel waves. Logical examinations concerning the pervasiveness and qualities of rebel waves in the district look to demystify the thought of unexplained peculiarities. Understanding the elements of rebel waves is fundamental for creating security measures and navigational procedures to relieve their effect on sea exercises.

The continuous investigation of the disaster areas inside the Bermuda Triangle has disclosed authentic antiquities as well as experiences into the circumstances that prompted their destruction. By concentrating on the destruction and leading criminological investigations, specialists can remake the occasions encompassing the sinking or vanishing of vessels. This approach takes into consideration a more proof based comprehension of the episodes related with the Bermuda Triangle.

The disaster areas inside the Bermuda Triangle act as submerged time cases, safeguarding components of sea history and giving unmistakable connections to the past. The investigation of these disaster areas contributes not exclusively to disentangling the secrets of explicit episodes yet additionally to a more extensive comprehension of verifiable route, shipping lanes, and mechanical headways in oceanic investigation. The disaster areas are basic to the sea legacy of the district, and continuous endeavors to record and moderate these destinations guarantee that they stay open for people in the future.

Notwithstanding the land and maritime variables, the human component of oceanic exercises inside the Bermuda Triangle is a urgent part of logical examination. Understanding human way of behaving, dynamic cycles, and the effect of mental elements on route is fundamental for grasping the difficulties looked by sailors. Exploring through the Bermuda Triangle requires a blend of expertise, experience, and the capacity to go with educated choices in the face regarding dynamic and once in a while erratic circumstances.

Human mistake, frequently disregarded in the stories of secretive vanishings, can assume a huge part in oceanic occurrences inside the Bermuda Triangle. Factors like weariness, stress, and misconceptions in exploring through testing waters can add to mishaps. By integrating the human component into logical examinations, specialists expect to foster methodologies for improving preparation, choice emotionally supportive networks, and wellbeing measures to diminish the gamble of episodes in the locale.

The logical examination of the Bermuda Triangle reaches out past the limits of the actual locale, including more extensive conversations about sea security, crisis reaction, and global collaboration. Examples gained from concentrating on the difficulties of the Bermuda Triangle can illuminate best practices for oceanic route internationally. The district fills in as a proving ground for systems and innovations pointed toward upgrading the security and versatility of oceanic exercises in different and complex conditions.

The continuous logical examinations concerning the Bermuda Triangle have changed the locale from a domain of legend and secret to a subject of extensive review. Topographical highlights, maritime elements, and human variables are vital parts of this logical request, revealing insight into the real essence of the risks looked by sailors and pilots inside the Bermuda Triangle. The planning of ocean bottom geology, the investigation of wrecks, and the assessment of human way of behaving add to a diverse comprehension that goes past hair-raising stories.

As exploration proceeds, the Bermuda Triangle turns into an image of verifiable episodes as well as of the intricacies intrinsic in exploring the world's seas. The coordination of logical information, mechanical headways, and illustrations from oceanic history encourages an all encompassing way to deal with guaranteeing security and versatility in sea exercises. The continuous investigation of the Bermuda Triangle welcomes a proceeded with cooperation between researchers, pilgrims, and oceanic experts, expecting to demystify the district and add to the more extensive comprehension of the difficulties presented by the vast ocean.

3.3 Debunking myths and exploring the real-life events behind the mystery.

Exposing legends and investigating the genuine occasions behind the secret of the Bermuda Triangle requires a cautious assessment of verifiable occurrences, logical clarifications, and the getting through charm of the unexplored world. The Bermuda Triangle, frequently alluded to as "Satan's Triangle," has been saturated with legend and hypothesis for a really long time, enthralling the public's creative mind with stories of secretive vanishings and unexplained peculiarities. In any case, a more intensive glance at current realities and logical examinations uncovers a more judicious and grounded comprehension of the district.

One of the getting through fantasies related with the Bermuda Triangle is that it is a particular and distinct region on the guide with fixed limits. Actually, the expression "Bermuda Triangle" isn't formally acknowledged by the U.S. government or any global sea association. The limits of the alleged triangle are inexactly characterized, commonly incorporating a region between Miami (Florida, USA), Bermuda, and San Juan (Puerto Rico). The absence of exact limits has prompted equivocalness in crediting episodes to the Bermuda Triangle, adding to the fantasy's persona.

The legend of the Bermuda Triangle acquired noticeable quality during the twentieth 100 years, energized by shocking stories and records of strange vanishings. One of the earliest and most notable episodes connected to the Bermuda Triangle is the vanishing of Flight 19 in December 1945. This unit of five U.S. Naval force aircraft evaporated during a normal preparation mission, and the ensuing pursuit and salvage mission likewise brought about the vanishing of a salvage plane. The conditions encompassing Flight 19 have been sensationalized, crediting the occurrence to paranormal or extraterrestrial powers.

Nonetheless, a more reasonable investigation of the Flight 19 episode focuses to navigational blunders, fuel weariness, and testing weather patterns as probable clarifications. The unit's chief became bewildered, driving the planes off kilter and into the immense region of the vast sea. The vanishing of the salvage plane can be ascribed to comparable variables, underscoring the difficulties of route and correspondence during unfriendly circumstances. While the tale of Flight 19 is many times refered to as a foundation of Bermuda Triangle folklore, a more dull assessment uncovers conceivable clarifications established in known factors.

The oceanic episodes related with the Bermuda Triangle likewise add to its persona. One such case is the vanishing of the SS Marine Sulfur Sovereign, a big hauler that evaporated in 1963 while on the way to Norfolk, Virginia. The vessel's vanishing prompted hypotheses about submerged peculiarities or extraterrestrial association.

Notwithstanding, a thorough examination uncovered that the SS Marine Sulfur Sovereign was inadequately kept up with, and its primary honesty probably split the difference. The vessel probably surrendered to the difficult atmospheric conditions it experienced during its excursion.

Another eminent occurrence is the sinking of the freight transport SS El Faro in 2015 during Storm Joaquin. The terrible occasion brought about the deficiency of all group individuals and powered conversations about the Bermuda Triangle's supposed risks. Notwithstanding, an exhaustive examination by the Public Transportation Wellbeing Board (NTSB) established that the sinking was fundamentally because of the skipper's choice to cruise excessively near the storm, misjudging the vessel's weakness to the extreme weather patterns.

The assessment of these genuine episodes inside the Bermuda Triangle features the significance of isolating truth from fiction. While the area has encountered sea and airborne mishaps, ascribing them exclusively to baffling or heavenly powers is unwarranted. All things considered, these occurrences frequently include a blend of navigational difficulties, unfavorable weather patterns, human blunder, and, at times, vessel or airplane related issues.

Logical examinations concerning the normal peculiarities inside the Bermuda Triangle add to exposing fantasies and dispersing the atmosphere of secret. The Bay Stream, a strong sea momentum coursing through the locale, is much of the time embroiled in the Bermuda Triangle's standing. The Bay Stream makes quick and warm maritime ebbs and flows, affecting the locale's hydrodynamics. While it can make testing ocean conditions, its belongings are surely known and not restrictive to the Bermuda Triangle.

Meteorological peculiarities, including typhoons and waterspouts, are normal in the Atlantic Sea and add to the district's climate elements. The Bermuda Triangle's area in a typhoon inclined zone improves the probability of experiencing serious climate, which can present critical dangers to oceanic and ethereal exercises. In any case, these weather conditions are essential for the regular environment of the locale and not characteristic of secretive or pernicious powers at play.

The geographical highlights of the ocean bottom inside the Bermuda Triangle, including remote ocean channels and submerged edges, have been investigated to figure out their possible effect on sea exercises. While these highlights add intricacy to the locale's submerged scene, they are not interesting to the Bermuda Triangle and don't add to baffling vanishings. The investigation of bathymetry and submerged geology helps with appreciating the difficulties looked by vessels exploring through the area however doesn't uphold otherworldly clarifications.

Maverick waves, frequently refered to in conversations about the Bermuda Triangle, are particularly huge and unforeseen maritime waves. While their reality is logically approved, crediting their event exclusively to the Bermuda Triangle is deceiving.

Rebel waves can happen in different regions of the planet seas and are a consequence of explicit maritime and air conditions. Their commonness inside the Bermuda Triangle is steady with worldwide examples and doesn't demonstrate a restricted peculiarity.

The investigation of the disaster areas inside the Bermuda Triangle gives significant bits of knowledge into the authentic setting of oceanic exercises in the locale. These disaster areas act as unmistakable proof of past occurrences and add to a more nuanced comprehension of the difficulties looked by vessels exploring through the area. Through logical investigation and submerged prehistoric studies, scientists gain an extensive perspective on the circumstances that prompted the disaster areas, exposing the idea of puzzling powers causing their downfall.

The human component in oceanic and flying route inside the Bermuda Triangle is a basic perspective frequently eclipsed by thrilling stories. The mental elements affecting independent direction, the difficulties of exploring through caught up with delivery paths, and the effect of pressure and weariness on teams all add to the intricacies of sea exercises. By recognizing the human aspect, logical examinations expect to further develop security measures, preparing conventions, and correspondence frameworks to diminish the gamble of occurrences in the district.

While the Bermuda Triangle stays an image of secret and interest, mainstream researchers keeps on demystifying the district through proof based examination and investigation. The appeal of the obscure, combined with the human interest with riddles, has propagated the fantasy of the Bermuda Triangle. Notwithstanding, a levelheaded and logical assessment uncovers a more complicated and multi-layered reality that includes normal powers, navigational difficulties, and the intricacies of oceanic investigation.

The persevering through interest with the Bermuda Triangle isn't just about exposing fantasies yet additionally about grasping the more extensive setting of sea investigation and the intricacies of the vast ocean. The secret encompassing the Bermuda Triangle has endured incompletely because of the human inclination to credit heavenly or uncommon clarifications to peculiarities that are not promptly perceived. In any case, the logical examination applied to the district disentangles the layers of legend and falsehood, offering a more nuanced viewpoint.

One variable that has added to the perseverance of the Bermuda Triangle legend is media emotionalism. The enhancement of secretive vanishings and the depiction of the district as a "risk zone" in mainstream society have sustained the thought of a powerful or evil power at play. The force of narrating, combined with the visual appeal of an indistinct three-sided region on maps, has filled the public's creative mind and added to the getting through persona of the Bermuda Triangle.

The charm of the obscure has consistently enthralled human interest, and the Bermuda Triangle addresses a current mystery in the time of trend setting innovation. In spite of the accessibility of logical clarifications and proof, the possibility of a locale where ships and planes evaporate without a follow keeps on catching the public's interest. The mental part of the secret, established in the apprehension about the obscure and the charm of the unexplained, adds to the persevering through notoriety of the Bermuda Triangle as a subject of conversation and hypothesis.

The exposing of fantasies encompassing the Bermuda Triangle isn't expected to lessen the meaning of the district's verifiable occurrences. Genuine misfortunes including the deficiency of vessels and lives merit regard and recognition. By embracing a logical methodology, scientists plan to respect the memory of the people who died in the Bermuda Triangle by revealing reality behind the episodes and dispersing unwarranted fantasies.

The continuous investigation of the Bermuda Triangle fills a double need of unwinding verifiable secrets and progressing logical information about the difficulties of oceanic route. As specialists dive into the disaster areas and relics inside the locale, they add to a developing comprehension of the mechanical, navigational, and human parts of past oceanic exercises. This information, thusly, illuminates contemporary sea rehearses and underscores the significance of constant improvement in wellbeing measures and crisis reaction conventions.

Logical examinations concerning the Bermuda Triangle additionally highlight the more extensive meaning of grasping Earth's seas. The difficulties looked by vessels in this district are not detached; they mirror the intricacies inborn in exploring the world's oceans. The Inlet Stream, submerged geology, and weather conditions inside the Bermuda Triangle are microcosms of the bigger maritime elements that influence worldwide sea exercises. By concentrating on this particular locale, researchers gain bits of knowledge that can be applied to improve security measures and route methodologies in different regions of the planet.

The exposing of fantasies and the investigation of genuine occasions behind the secret of the Bermuda Triangle address an excursion toward a more educated and levelheaded comprehension of the locale. Established researchers, students of history, and travelers cooperatively add to unwinding the intricacies of the Bermuda Triangle, dispersing exciting stories, and encouraging a more profound appreciation for the difficulties of oceanic investigation. While the charm of the obscure may persevere, the utilization of proof based approaches permits us to explore the waters of the Bermuda Triangle with a more clear figuring out, isolating reality from fiction as we continued looking for information and investigation.

Chapter 4

The Sunken City of Heracleion
Lost Treasures Revealed

The lowered vestiges of the old city of Heracleion, otherwise called Thonis, have extended stayed perhaps of the most spellbinding archeological disclosure in the domain of submerged investigation. Situated at the mouth of the Nile Waterway in the Mediterranean Ocean, this once-energetic port city assumed a pivotal part in the sea shipping lanes of the old world. The tale of its vanishing and the ensuing disclosure of its submerged fortunes offers an entrancing look into the secrets of the past.

Heracleion flourished as a clamoring center of exchange and social trade from the sixth to the fourth century BCE. The city, accepted to have been established around the eighth century BCE, filled in as a door among Egypt and the Mediterranean, encouraging associations between different developments. As a vital port of section, Heracleion worked with the exchange of products going from valuable metals and materials to colorful flavors and relics. The city's essential area made it an indispensable place for trade and strategy, molding its way of life as a cosmopolitan city.

The specific conditions encompassing the submergence of Heracleion remained covered in secret for quite a long time. Antiquated texts and engravings made reference to the city's continuous decay because of catastrophic events, including tremors and rising ocean levels. Verifiable records additionally noticed Heracleion's importance in strict functions, with its fabulous sanctuaries committed to divinities like Amun-Gereb and Khonsu. Notwithstanding, as the hundreds of years passed, the city's presence blurred into haziness, and its area turned into the stuff of legend.

The re-disclosure of Heracleion started in the mid 21st 100 years, when submerged archeologists left on a mission to uncover the secrets lying underneath the waters close to the Egyptian shoreline. The aggressive endeavor, drove by French paleologist Franck Goddio, involved the utilization of cutting edge marine review advances like sonar and attractive imaging. These state of the art apparatuses empowered specialists to plan the submerged landscape and distinguish likely archeological destinations.

In the year 2000, the group's endeavors proved to be fruitful as they revealed the principal leftovers of what might later be affirmed as Heracleion. Lowered underneath layers of residue and marine flotsam and jetsam, the city's sculptures, sanctuaries, and different designs started to rise up out of the profundities. The archeological disclosures illustrated a city that had capitulated to the powers of nature and time, protecting its fortunes underneath the sandy seabed.

One of the most noteworthy elements of Heracleion's submerged scene was the presence of titanic sculptures, some arriving at levels of more than 16 feet. These gigantic models portrayed gods, pharaohs, and legendary figures, highlighting the city's rich strict and social legacy. The sheer scale and creativity of these sculptures mirrored the greatness that once characterized Heracleion as a focal point of other-worldly love and imaginative articulation.

The submerged unearthings likewise uncovered the remainders of an organization of channels and harbors, giving bits of knowledge into the city's high level designing and oceanic foundation. Heracleion's design exhibited a very much arranged metropolitan climate, complete with sanctuaries, local locations, and business regions. The fastidious association of the city's designs indicated a refined society that blossomed with exchange, tact, and social trade.

As archeologists carefully uncovered curios from the submerged city, a gold mine of social relics became known. The seabed yielded a variety of curios, including ceramics, gems, coins, and strict images. These tracks down not just given unmistakable associations with the day to day routines of Heracleion's occupants yet additionally offered significant pieces of information about the city's financial exercises and exchange organizations.

The strict meaning of Heracleion was additionally highlighted by the revelation of very much saved sanctuary structures enhanced with mind boggling carvings and engravings. These sanctuaries filled in as focuses of love for the antiquated Egyptians, with customs and functions directed to respect the divinities accepted to administer the city's destiny. The submerged investigation of these consecrated locales permitted scientists to sort out the profound practices that once characterized Heracleion.

Quite possibly of the most notorious construction found in Heracleion was the terrific sanctuary of Amun-Gereb, a god related with ripeness, horticulture, and development. The sanctuary's giant sculptures and lavish sections mirrored the structural ability of the old Egyptians. The mind boggling carvings on the sanctuary walls recounted accounts of strict functions, offering a window into the other-worldly existence of Heracleion's occupants.

The relics recuperated from Heracleion shed light on the city's set of experiences as well as given significant bits of knowledge into the more extensive social and financial elements of the antiquated world. The city's job as a flourishing exchange community became obvious through the revelation of relics starting from different districts, including Greece, Phoenicia, and the more extensive Mediterranean. These discoveries verified Heracleion's status as a mixture of different impacts and a pivotal hub in the oceanic shipping lanes of days of yore.

The indented city's rediscovery likewise brought up issues about the variables that prompted its death. While cataclysmic events were accepted to play had an impact, continuous examination tried to disentangle the intricate interchange of land, ecological, and anthropogenic variables that added to Heracleion's submergence. The investigation of silt layers and center examples meant to recreate the ecological circumstances that won during the city's downfall, giving a comprehensive comprehension of the powers at play.

The conservation of Heracleion's relics represented a novel test as openness to air and daylight could prompt fast weakening. Protection endeavors were executed to painstakingly concentrate, report, and safeguard the recuperated things. The fastidious interaction included the utilization of specific procedures to settle and safeguard sensitive materials, guaranteeing that the fortunes of Heracleion could be imparted to people in the future.

The meaning of Heracleion reached out past its archeological and authentic worth. The indented city offered a substantial connection to the old past, permitting scientists to sort out stories that rose above time. The curios and designs that lay secret underneath the waves filled in as quiet observers to the accomplishments, yearnings, and difficulties of a former period. The investigation of Heracleion welcomed examination on the fleetingness of human advancements and the flexibility of social legacy notwithstanding regular powers.

The disclosures from Heracleion reverberated in the domain of sea prehistoric studies, featuring the potential for additional revelations underneath the world's seas and oceans.

The submerged investigation of lowered urban areas and old wrecks opened roads for understanding the interconnected accounts of waterfront civic establishments and the urgent pretended by sea exchange. Heracleion remained as a demonstration of the untold stories anticipating revelation underneath the waves, welcoming wayfarers and scientists to unwind the secrets of other lowered civic establishments.

The submerged city of Heracleion not just dazzles the creative mind through its archeological fortunes yet in addition prompts consideration on the more extensive ramifications of oceanic paleontology. The submerged investigation of Heracleion is symbolic of the potential for rediscovery and disclosure that lies underneath the world's seas. As innovation propels and our comprehension of submerged prehistoric studies develops, there is a rising consciousness of the rich embroidery of mankind's set of experiences ready to be revealed underneath the waves.

The investigation of Heracleion adds to how we might interpret the interconnectedness of old human advancements and the critical pretended by sea exchange molding social scenes. The ancient rarities recuperated from the depressed city recount accounts of business, social trade, and strict practices that rose above territorial limits. Heracleion's situation as an oceanic junction highlights the significance of seaside urban communities in working with the progression of merchandise, thoughts, and creative impacts across the old world.

The exchange networks that merged in Heracleion united assorted societies and added to the city's cosmopolitan person. The curios recuperated from the seabed incorporate Egyptian relics as well as things from Greece, Phoenicia, and other Mediterranean areas. The presence of imported products and the trading of social practices feature the powerful connections that described Heracleion as a blend of impacts.

The submerged investigation of Heracleion is likewise a demonstration of the versatility of social legacy notwithstanding ecological difficulties. The city's decay and possible submergence were reasonable impacted by a blend of elements, including rising ocean levels, seismic action, and human exercises. By concentrating on the ecological circumstances that prompted Heracleion's end, scientists gain experiences into the mind boggling exchange of normal and anthropogenic powers that shape waterfront scenes.

The conservation of Heracleion's antiques, notwithstanding hundreds of years underneath the ocean, addresses the getting through nature of specific materials and the defensive characteristics of the submerged climate. The seabed, with its absence of openness to air and daylight, established a climate helpful for the protection of natural and inorganic materials. The careful preservation endeavors applied to the recuperated curios expect to guarantee that the fortunes of Heracleion are protected for people in the future.

Heracleion's fantastic sanctuaries, decorated with many-sided carvings and committed to respected gods, give a window into the profound existence of the old Egyptians. The submerged investigation of these hallowed destinations permits analysts to reproduce strict services, customs, and the meaning of the city's sanctuaries in the regular routines of its occupants. The lowered strict designs contribute not exclusively to the comprehension of Heracleion's social practices yet additionally to more extensive conversations about the job of religion in antiquated beach front urban areas.

Past its authentic and archeological importance, the investigation of Heracleion brings up issues about the effect of environmental change and ocean level ascent on seaside networks since forever ago. While the submergence of Heracleion might have been affected by normal land processes, the equals with contemporary worries about rising ocean levels and beach front disintegration are clear. The investigation of antiquated beach front urban communities gives important experiences into the drawn out elements of waterfront scenes and the manners by which human social orders have adjusted to ecological changes.

The mechanical headways that empowered the revelation and investigation of Heracleion address a change in perspective in submerged prehistoric studies. The utilization of cutting edge marine review innovations, including sonar and attractive imaging, permitted specialists to plan the submerged territory with phenomenal detail. These apparatuses worked with the ID of lowered structures as well as supported the preparation of designated unearthings, limiting the effect on the sensitive submerged climate.

The use of advanced mechanics and remotely worked vehicles (ROVs) further upgraded the accuracy and proficiency of submerged investigation. These mechanical frameworks permitted archeologists to arrive at profundities and explore complex submerged scenes that were beforehand out of reach. The utilization of ROVs furnished with cameras and sensors empowered constant perception and documentation of the submerged locales, giving an abundance of visual information for resulting examination.

The cooperative energy among innovation and human aptitude in the investigation of Heracleion features the cooperative idea of contemporary archeological undertakings. Interdisciplinary groups, including archeologists, sea life researchers, traditionalists, and designers, cooperate to open the mysteries of lowered civic establishments. The coordination of different mastery guarantees a comprehensive way to deal with submerged investigation, integrating logical thoroughness, protection morals, and a profound appreciation for social legacy.

The disclosures from Heracleion likewise add to continuous conversations about the moral contemplations of submerged prehistoric studies. The investigation and uncovering of lowered locales require a fragile harmony between the quest for information and the conservation of social legacy.

Archeologists face moral difficulties connected with site unsettling influence, ancient rarity preservation, and the expected effect of human exercises on submerged biological systems. The advancement of rules and moral structures for submerged prehistoric studies looks to address these contemplations and advance capable investigation and documentation.

The proceeded with investigation of Heracleion and comparable submerged locales highlights the significance of global cooperation in the field of sea antiquarianism. The submerged city's importance reaches out past public lines, and the protection of its fortunes requires an aggregate exertion. Cooperative drives including analysts, establishments, and legislative organizations intend to share information, assets, and best practices for the maintainable investigation and security of lowered social legacy.

The charm of lowered urban communities and their secret fortunes resounds with researchers and archeologists as well as with the more extensive public. The disclosure of Heracleion caught the world's consideration, starting interest in the secrets lying underneath the ocean. The public's interest with submerged prehistoric studies mirrors a general interest previously and the untold stories that might be ready to be uncovered underneath the waves.

The submerged city of Heracleion, with its buried fortunes uncovered through cutting edge submerged investigation, remains as an image of the potential for disclosure and disclosure that lies underneath the world's seas. The investigation of Heracleion contributes not exclusively to how we might interpret old civilizations and sea exchange yet in addition to more extensive conversations about environmental change, social legacy safeguarding, and the moral contemplations of submerged paleohistory. As innovation proceeds to progress and our appreciation for the interconnectedness of mankind's set of experiences develops, the investigation of lowered urban communities offers a passage to the secrets of the past, ready to be revealed underneath the ocean.

4.1 Unveiling the submerged city of Heracleion off the coast of Egypt.

The divulging of the lowered city of Heracleion, arranged off the shore of Egypt at the mouth of the Nile Waterway, addresses a stupendous section in the records of submerged paleontology. This old city, otherwise called Thonis, remained as a clamoring oceanic center for a really long time, interfacing different civilizations through exchange, culture, and strict trade. The tale of its submergence and resulting rediscovery offers an enamoring story that unwinds the secrets of the past while revealing insight into the intricacies of old oceanic civic establishments.

Heracleion's verifiable importance is established in its essential area and critical job in sea shipping lanes during the late first thousand years BCE. Laid out around the eighth century BCE, the city thrived as an entryway among Egypt and the Mediterranean, encouraging a cosmopolitan climate that invited impacts from different societies.

Heracleion's thriving was unpredictably attached to its sea associations, permitting it to turn into an essential place for trade, strategy, and social communications.

The city's conspicuousness is obvious in authentic records and engravings that feature its financial ability and strict importance. Sanctuaries devoted to loved gods, including Amun-Gereb and Khonsu, decorated the scene, filling in as focuses of love and profound direction. The glory of these strict designs, combined with the richness of Heracleion's engineering, mirrored the city's remaining as a flourishing metropolitan community.

Notwithstanding, Heracleion's destiny took a sensational turn, set apart by a continuous decay and inevitable submergence underneath the waters of the Mediterranean. The specific explanations behind the city's destruction stayed perplexing for a really long time, with old texts implying cataclysmic events, including quakes and rising ocean levels, as expected contributing variables. As the ways of the world clouded Heracleion's presence, it blurred into lack of definition, turning into a subject of hypothesis and legend.

The journey to divulge Heracleion's secrets picked up speed in the mid 21st century when a group of submerged archeologists, drove by French wayfarer Franck

Goddio, left on an aggressive mission to find and investigate the depressed city. Utilizing state of the art marine study advancements, including sonar and attractive imaging, the group fastidiously planned the submerged territory off the Egyptian coast. The utilization of cutting edge apparatuses empowered the recognizable proof of expected archeological destinations underneath the seabed.

In the year 2000, the finish of these endeavors prompted a weighty revelation as the lowered remainders of Heracleion started to rise up out of the profundities. Gigantic sculptures, sanctuary designs, and relics that had lain concealed for quite a long time materialized, giving a brief look into the dynamic city that once flourished along the Nile Delta. The disclosure of Heracleion enthralled the world, catching the minds of researchers, archeologists, and the public the same.

One of the most striking elements of Heracleion's submerged scene was the presence of monster sculptures that arrived at levels of north of 16 feet. These fantastic models, portraying pharaohs, divinities, and legendary figures, displayed the imaginative and structural ability of the old Egyptians. The sheer scale and multifaceted design of these sculptures highlighted the magnificence that characterized Heracleion's strict and social scene.

The submerged investigation likewise uncovered the remainders of a refined organization of channels and harbors, giving experiences into the city's sea foundation. Heracleion's format, set apart by all around arranged metropolitan spaces, sanctuaries, and business locale, uncovered a high level comprehension of city arranging.

The unpredictable association of the city's designs indicated a general public that blossomed with exchange, navigational skill, and social variety.

As archeologists carefully uncovered the seabed, a gold mine of curios arose, going from ceramics and gems to strict images and coins. These relics not just given substantial associations with the regular routines of Heracleion's occupants yet in addition offered significant hints about the city's monetary exercises and exchange organizations. The variety of curios, including things of unfamiliar beginning, addressed Heracleion's job as a mixture of societies and a focal point of oceanic exchange.

The strict meaning of Heracleion was clear in the revelation of very much protected sanctuary structures enhanced with complex carvings and engravings. The fabulous sanctuary of Amun-Gereb, specifically, remained as a demonstration of the city's profound life. The sanctuary's goliath sculptures and luxurious segments mirrored the strict intensity that penetrated Heracleion, and the carvings on its walls given looks into the functions and ceremonies that occurred inside.

The rediscovery of Heracleion provoked a reconsideration of its verifiable and social significance. The city's cosmopolitan nature, set apart by the assembly of various developments, tested assumptions about the insularity of old social orders. Heracleion's job as a sea junction offered a nuanced comprehension of social trade and interconnected chronicles, stressing the reliance of waterfront urban communities in the old world.

The investigation of Heracleion's end turned into a point of convergence for specialists trying to unwind the complicated elements that prompted the city's submergence. While cataclysmic events were viewed as contributing variables, continuous examinations planned to reproduce the natural circumstances that won during Heracleion's downfall. The examination of silt layers and center examples looked to give a complete comprehension of the land, climatic, and anthropogenic powers at play.

The protection of Heracleion's curios represented a novel test, as openness to air and daylight could prompt fast decay. Preservation endeavors were carried out to painstakingly concentrate, report, and protect the recuperated things. The careful cycle included the utilization of particular strategies to balance out and safeguard sensitive materials, guaranteeing that the fortunes of Heracleion could be examined and imparted to people in the future.

Heracleion's rediscovery not just revealed insight into the city's authentic setting yet additionally brought up issues about the effect of environmental change and ocean level ascent on seaside developments from the beginning of time. While the submergence of Heracleion was affected by normal geographical cycles, the equals with contemporary worries about rising ocean levels and seaside disintegration were clear.

The investigation of old waterfront urban areas gives significant experiences into the drawn out elements of seaside scenes and the manners by which human social orders have adjusted to ecological changes.

The uncovering of Heracleion's lowered fortunes additionally featured the groundbreaking job of innovation in submerged paleontology. The utilization of cutting edge marine overview innovations, like sonar and attractive imaging, altered the investigation of lowered locales. These instruments empowered scientists to plan submerged territories with extraordinary accuracy, directing designated unearthings and limiting the effect on fragile conditions.

The sending of remotely worked vehicles (ROVs) furnished with cameras and sensors further upgraded the effectiveness of submerged investigation. These mechanical frameworks permitted archeologists to arrive at profundities and explore complex submerged scenes that were already out of reach. The constant perception and documentation worked with by ROVs gave an abundance of visual information for resulting examination, adding to a more far reaching comprehension of lowered locales.

The joint effort among innovation and human aptitude in the investigation of Heracleion highlighted the interdisciplinary idea of contemporary archeological undertakings. Groups of archeologists, sea life researchers, protectionists, and designers worked cooperatively to open the privileged insights of lowered civilizations. The joining of different skill guaranteed an all encompassing way to deal with submerged investigation, integrating logical meticulousness, preservation morals, and a profound appreciation for social legacy.

Heracleion's disclosures resounded inside academic circles as well as caught the public's creative mind. The charm of lowered urban communities and their secret fortunes hit home for a worldwide crowd, starting interest in the secrets lying underneath the ocean. The rediscovery of Heracleion turned into an image of the unlimited marvels that may be ready to be uncovered underneath the outer layer of our planet's tremendous seas.

The disclosing of the lowered city of Heracleion not just gives a window into the old past yet in addition prompts reflections on the more extensive ramifications and meaning of oceanic paleohistory. The tale of Heracleion's rediscovery is a demonstration of the versatility of social legacy and the getting through charm of lowered civic establishments. As analysts keep on diving into the secrets of this depressed city, the investigation offers significant bits of knowledge into the interconnectedness of old social orders, the effect of ecological changes, and the extraordinary job of innovation in submerged prehistoric studies.

The cosmopolitan person of Heracleion, with its job as an oceanic intersection, challenges ordinary stories about the detachment of old civic establishments.

The combination of assorted societies in this submerged city addresses the ease and penetrability of social limits, accentuating the relationship of seaside urban communities in working with the progression of products, thoughts, and creative impacts across the antiquated world. The relics recuperated from Heracleion, including things of unfamiliar beginning, highlight the city's status as a blend of societies and a demonstration of the lavishness of oceanic exchange organizations.

The rediscovery of Heracleion likewise highlights the versatility of social legacy even with natural difficulties. While the specific reasons for Heracleion's submergence remain subjects of progressing research, the equals with contemporary worries about rising ocean levels and environmental change are obvious. The investigation of old beach front urban communities, like Heracleion, adds to a more profound comprehension of the drawn out elements of waterfront scenes and the manners by which human social orders have adjusted to natural changes over centuries.

Heracleion's great sanctuaries, decorated with many-sided carvings and devoted to loved gods, give a brief look into the profound existence of the old Egyptians. The submerged investigation of these holy destinations permits analysts to remake strict services, customs, and the meaning of the city's sanctuaries in the regular routines of its occupants. The lowered strict designs contribute not exclusively to the comprehension of Heracleion's social practices yet additionally to more extensive conversations about the job of religion in antiquated beach front urban communities and the development of strict convictions over the long haul.

The investigation of Heracleion's death envelops a multidisciplinary approach, joining topographical, climatic, and anthropogenic elements. Residue layers and center examples taken from the submerged site offer pieces of information about the natural circumstances that won during the city's downfall. By disentangling the mind boggling exchange of regular and human-initiated powers, scientists expect to develop a thorough story that contextualizes Heracleion's submergence inside the more extensive system of old waterfront elements.

Protection endeavors applied to the curios recuperated from Heracleion represent the sensitive harmony between the quest for information and the conservation of social legacy. The fastidious extraction, documentation, and safeguarding of these things require a combination of customary archeological systems with current protection procedures. The test lies in shielding fragile materials as well as in creating feasible practices that guarantee the drawn out security of lowered social legacy.

The disclosing of Heracleion off the shore of Egypt encapsulates the groundbreaking effect of innovation on submerged prehistoric studies. High level marine overview advances, like sonar and attractive imaging, reformed the investigation of lowered destinations, empowering scientists to plan submerged landscapes with exceptional accuracy.

The utilization of remotely worked vehicles (ROVs) furnished with cameras and sensors further improved the productivity of submerged investigation, giving ongoing perception and documentation of the lowered city.

The cooperative idea of contemporary submerged prehistoric studies, as confirmed in the investigation of Heracleion, features the significance of interdisciplinary groups. Archeologists, sea life researchers, moderates, and specialists cooperate to explore the difficulties presented by submerged conditions and open the insider facts of lowered developments. The coordination of different skill guarantees an all encompassing methodology that consolidates logical meticulousness, protection morals, and a significant regard for social legacy.

Heracleion's rediscovery spellbound researchers and scientists as well as the worldwide public. The interest with lowered urban communities and their secret fortunes mirrors a general interest before and the secrets that lie underneath the ocean. The investigation of Heracleion turned into an image of the vast potential outcomes anticipating revelation underneath the outer layer of our planet's seas, encouraging a reestablished revenue in oceanic paleohistory and the investigation of lowered social legacy.

The disclosing of the lowered city of Heracleion off the shoreline of Egypt remains as an essential second in the domain of submerged prehistoric studies. The rediscovery of this old sea center point difficulties assumptions about the seclusion of old civic establishments and offers significant experiences into the interconnectedness of beach front urban areas. Heracleion's lowered fortunes enhance how we might interpret the past as well as add to progressing conversations about environmental change, the flexibility of social legacy, and the groundbreaking job of innovation in opening the mysteries of the ocean. As analysts keep on investigating the secrets of Heracleion and other lowered destinations, the appeal of the submerged world calls, welcoming us to disentangle the untold stories that stay concealed underneath the waves.

4.2 Archaeological discoveries and the use of underwater technologies to explore and document the ruins.

The field of submerged paleohistory has gone through a progressive change in late many years, with archeological disclosures underneath the waves revealing new insight into old civic establishments and oceanic history. The utilization of cutting edge submerged innovations plays had an essential impact in investigating and recording lowered ruins, revealing an abundance of curios and designs that were beforehand out of reach. This story investigates the collaboration between archeological disclosures and the state of the art advancements utilized in submerged investigation, featuring the extraordinary effect on how we might interpret the past.

One of the most astounding parts of submerged paleohistory is its capacity to divulge stowed away sections of mankind's set of experiences that lie underneath the outer layer of seas, oceans, and lakes. As earthbound prehistoric studies centers around land-based locales, submerged archaic exploration stretches out the degree to incorporate lowered scenes, antiquated wrecks, and depressed urban areas. These submerged conditions go about as time cases, protecting relics and designs in a strikingly very much saved state because of the shortfall of openness to air, daylight, and earthly components.

The investigation of lowered ruins frequently starts with the ID of possible destinations through a blend of verifiable exploration, satellite symbolism, and marine overviews. Waterfront locales, riverbeds, and realized sea shipping lanes become central focuses for examination. When a promising region is recognized, high level marine review innovations become possibly the most important factor to plan the submerged landscape with accuracy.

Sonar innovation has turned into a foundation in submerged paleontology, empowering scientists to make definite three-layered guides of the ocean bottom. Side-examine sonar, specifically, produces sound waves that bob off the ocean bottom and submerged objects, giving high-goal pictures of the lowered scene. These sonar pictures uncover peculiarities, like expected archeological designs or wrecks, provoking further examination.

Attractive imaging is one more amazing asset in the submerged paleontologist's weapons store. By recognizing varieties in the World's attractive field brought about by lowered designs or articles, analysts can distinguish likely archeological locales. This innovation is especially helpful in planning antiquated ports, harbors, and the leftovers of wooden designs that may not be apparent through customary overview techniques.

When potential destinations are recognized through these overviews, the following stage includes designated unearthings and investigations. Remotely Worked Vehicles (ROVs) and Independent Submerged Vehicles (AUVs) have become imperative in such manner. These automated frameworks are furnished with cameras, sensors, and at times mechanical arms for fragile tasks. They permit archeologists to arrive at profundities and explore complex submerged scenes that were once blocked off, giving continuous perception and documentation of lowered destinations.

The cooperative energy among innovation and human aptitude is obvious in the revelation and investigation of lowered ruins. The utilization of ROVs and AUVs empowers archeologists to direct exact, non-meddling examinations. This is especially essential for the protection of fragile curios and designs, as conventional exhuming techniques can be testing and possibly harming in submerged conditions.

One of the noticeable instances of submerged prehistoric studies' groundbreaking effect is the revelation and investigation of the lowered city of Heracleion off the shoreline of Egypt. Utilizing progressed marine review advancements, including sonar and attractive imaging, French excavator Franck Goddio and his group found the lowered remains of Heracleion in the mid 21st hundred years. The utilization of ROVs took into account the fastidious removal and documentation of enormous sculptures, sanctuary designs, and curios that had been secret underneath the Mediterranean for a really long time.

The investigation of Heracleion uncovered a city that once flourished as an indispensable place for sea exchange and social trade. Goliath sculptures, some arriving at more than 16 feet in level, portrayed pharaohs and gods, displaying the city's imaginative and engineering magnificence. The remainders of sanctuaries devoted to Amun-Gereb and different gods gave experiences into the strict acts of the antiquated Egyptians. The utilization of cutting edge innovations worked with the disclosure of Heracleion as well as guaranteed the conservation of its lowered fortunes for people in the future.

Wrecks, frequently alluded to as time containers of the past, have been a point of convergence for submerged archeologists. The disclosure and investigation of old wrecks offer an exceptional look into nautical societies, shipping lanes, and sea innovations of former periods. One of the most praised models is the Antikythera wreck, found off the shore of the Greek island of Antikythera in the mid twentieth 100 years.

The Antikythera wreck, dated to the primary century BCE, yielded an exceptional mother lode of curios, including bronze sculptures, amphorae, and the well known Antikythera Component. This modern mechanical gadget is viewed as perhaps of the earliest simple PC, fit for anticipating galactic positions and obscurations. The submerged removal of the Antikythera wreck included spearheading jumping methods and later, the utilization of cutting edge innovations like ROVs to explore the tricky profundities.

Lately, headways in submerged antiquarianism have extended past conventional strategies to incorporate 3D displaying and augmented reality (VR). These advances permit analysts to make vivid encounters that rejuvenate lowered locales for the two researchers and the overall population. 3D displaying, produced from information gathered through sonar and photogrammetry, empowers the production of definite reproductions of submerged designs and relics.

Augmented reality applications give an extra layer of availability, permitting clients to investigate lowered ruins from the solace of their homes or instructive foundations. These computerized reproductions not just act as important exploration instruments for archeologists yet in addition democratize admittance to submerged legacy, cultivating a more extensive comprehension and enthusiasm for oceanic paleohistory.

The utilization of innovation in submerged paleohistory stretches out past the investigation stage to incorporate the protection and preservation of recuperated relics. Once uncovered, relics from lowered locales are much of the time in a fragile state because of their delayed openness to submerged conditions. Preservation endeavors include specific methods to settle, clean, and safeguard these curios to guarantee their drawn out conservation.

Electrolytic decrease, for instance, is a typical technique used to treat metal curios recuperated from submerged destinations. This cycle includes passing a low electrical flow through the relic while lowered in an answer, successfully eliminating erosion and encrustation. Natural materials, like wood or calfskin, go through a freeze-drying cycle to forestall crumbling. The outcome of these preservation endeavors is urgent in keeping up with the trustworthiness of antiquities and empowering further review.

While the headways in submerged advancements have opened new outskirts in archaic exploration, they likewise present moral contemplations and difficulties. Protection of the sensitive submerged climate is central, and specialists should explore the scarcely discernible difference among investigation and preservation. Rules and moral structures have been created to address concerns connected with site aggravation, ancient rarity preservation, and the likely effect of human exercises on submerged biological systems.

The worldwide idea of submerged paleontology requires global cooperation. Lowered legacy locales frequently rise above public lines, requiring composed endeavors among analysts, organizations, and administrative offices. Cooperative drives mean to share information, assets, and best practices for the supportable investigation and security of lowered social legacy.

The combination of innovation and submerged paleohistory has not just changed the manner in which we investigate and report lowered ruins yet has additionally widened how we might interpret mankind's set of experiences. The disclosures caused underneath the disturbances add to a more exhaustive story of old developments, sea exchange organizations, and nautical societies. The utilization of trend setting innovations guarantees that these revelations are made as well as protected for people in the future.

The reconciliation of innovation into submerged paleontology not just works with the investigation and documentation of lowered ruins yet additionally opens new roads for grasping the intricacies of antiquated social orders and their oceanic collaborations. The proceeded with progressions in submerged advances add to the extension of our insight about mankind's set of experiences, social trade, and the effect of ecological changes on beach front civic establishments.

One of the huge commitments of submerged prehistoric studies is its part in unwinding the sea exchange networks that associated antiquated human advancements.

Wrecks, specifically, act as important windows into marine societies and the products that were shipped across immense distances. The Belitung wreck, found off the bank of Indonesia, is a great representation of how submerged paleohistory has enhanced how we might interpret old shipping lanes.

The Belitung wreck, dated to the ninth 100 years, uncovered a freight of valuable ceramics, gold, silver, and different curios. The disclosure gave experiences into the oceanic Silk Street, an organization of shipping lanes that associated East Asia, South Asia, and the Center East. Through the careful exhuming and investigation of the boat's freight, scientists acquired a more profound comprehension of the items exchanged, social trades, and the financial elements of the time.

Past wrecks, the investigation of lowered urban areas offers an interesting viewpoint on the metropolitan communities that flourished along shores. Pavlopetri, situated off the bank of Greece, is one such lowered city that traces all the way back to the Bronze Age. The utilization of sonar planning and ROVs uncovered a very much arranged metropolitan settlement with roads, structures, and a complicated framework.

Pavlopetri's format difficulties regular ideas about the improvement of metropolitan focuses and features the timely arrangement and designing abilities of old social orders. The investigation of lowered urban areas adds to how we might interpret how waterfront networks adjusted to changing ecological circumstances, featuring the flexibility of human settlements despite normal difficulties.

The cooperative energy among innovation and paleohistory is especially obvious in the use of 3D displaying and computer generated reality (VR) to reproduce lowered conditions. These advanced recreations not just act as strong representation devices for analysts yet in addition offer vivid encounters for the general population. Virtual plunges into old wrecks or depressed urban areas give a feeling of investigation and disclosure, overcoming any barrier between established researchers and a more extensive crowd.

The utilization of VR additionally addresses the difficulties of openness related with submerged paleohistory. Many lowered destinations are situated at extensive profundities, making actual visits trying for analysts and fans. Virtual recreations democratize admittance to these destinations, permitting people from around the world to investigate and draw in with submerged legacy.

As innovation keeps on propelling, the potential for new disclosures underneath the waves grows. The utilization of Computerized reasoning (artificial intelligence) in dissecting huge datasets produced from submerged overviews offers a promising road for recognizing expected archeological destinations.

Man-made intelligence calculations can process and decipher sonar and attractive information, helping archeologists in pinpointing areas of premium for additional examination.

Besides, the combination of mechanical technology and simulated intelligence in submerged investigation can upgrade the proficiency and accuracy of archeological undertakings. Independent Submerged Vehicles (AUVs) furnished with simulated intelligence abilities can independently explore submerged conditions, dissect information progressively, and settle on conclusions about where to concentrate consideration. This degree of independence takes into account more designated and versatile investigation systems, advancing the utilization of assets and time.

The utilization of cutting edge innovations in submerged archaic exploration additionally reaches out to ecological checking and preservation endeavors. As environmental change presents dangers to lowered legacy locales, scientists utilize observing frameworks to follow changes in temperature, saltiness, and ocean levels. This information is pivotal for understanding the effect of environmental change on submerged archeological locales and creating methodologies for their assurance and conservation.

Be that as it may, the joining of innovation into submerged archaic exploration accompanies moral contemplations. The potential for business double-dealing, plundering, and harm to submerged locales raises worries about the protection of social legacy. The advancement of moral rules and global joint efforts looks to address these difficulties, guaranteeing that the investigation of lowered ruins is led mindfully and reasonably.

The collaboration between archeological revelations and submerged innovations has changed how we might interpret old civilizations and their connections with the oceanic climate. From wrecks to lowered urban communities, high level marine review advancements, ROVs, AUVs, 3D demonstrating, and simulated intelligence have become crucial apparatuses for scientists in the field of submerged archaic exploration. These advances not just empower the investigation of stowed away sections of mankind's set of experiences yet additionally add to the more extensive accounts of exchange, metropolitan turn of events, and social trade. As the field keeps on developing, the reconciliation of innovation guarantees further disclosures, extending the skylines of submerged investigation and advancing our enthusiasm for the lowered legacy that lies underneath the waves.

4.3 Insights into the historical and cultural significance of the rediscovered city.

The rediscovery of the lowered city of Heracleion off the shoreline of Egypt has given significant experiences into the verifiable and social embroidery of old developments, offering a charming story that rises above the limits of time.

As archeologists fastidiously uncover the leftovers of this once-flourishing city, the lowered remains of Heracleion unfurl a story of sea loftiness, social combination, and the perplexing exchange of different civic establishments along the Nile Delta.

The verifiable meaning of Heracleion is well established in its essential area and job as a sea center point during the late first thousand years BCE. Laid out around the eighth century BCE, the city thrived as a door among Egypt and the Mediterranean, cultivating a cosmopolitan climate that invited impacts from different societies. Heracleion's conspicuousness in oceanic shipping lanes made it an imperative place for trade, discretion, and social trade, molding its way of life as a junction of civilizations.

The archeological investigation of Heracleion has uncovered a cityscape set apart by terrific sanctuaries, titanic sculptures, and multifaceted building wonders. The magnificence of these designs addresses the richness and refinement of old Egyptian human advancement. Sanctuaries devoted to venerated divinities, including Amun-Gereb and Khonsu, enhanced the scene, filling in as focuses of love and otherworldly direction. The fantastic sculptures, a few overshadowing 16 feet in level, portrayed pharaohs, divinities, and legendary figures, exhibiting the creative ability of the old Egyptians.

The lowered city's engineering design and metropolitan arranging further confirm the high level comprehension of city association in antiquated times. Roads, squares, and locale planned with fastidious accuracy indicate a general public that esteemed request and usefulness. The remainders of an intricate organization of waterways and harbors highlight Heracleion's oceanic foundation, underlining job as a clamoring port city worked with exchange and social cooperations.

One of the most convincing parts of Heracleion's authentic importance lies in its social and strict variety. The city's cosmopolitan nature is obvious in the assembly of various civic establishments along its shores. The archeological discoveries incorporate curios of unfamiliar beginning, underlining the job of Heracleion as a blend where societies interlaced and thoughts coursed. This social variety challenges ordinary thoughts of antiquated social orders as confined elements, featuring the interconnectedness of seaside urban communities in the old world.

The strict meaning of Heracleion is appeared in the disclosure of very much protected sanctuary structures enhanced with mind boggling carvings and engravings. The excellent sanctuary of Amun-Gereb, specifically, remains as a demonstration of the profound existence of the old Egyptians. The epic sculptures, resplendent segments, and point by point carvings on the sanctuary walls give looks into the strict services, ceremonies, and convictions that saturated Heracleion's general public.

The lowered sanctuaries become entries to the past, offering bits of knowledge into the otherworldly practices that molded the existences of the city's occupants.

Heracleion's verifiable account additionally crosses with more extensive conversations about the oceanic shipping lanes and monetary elements of the old world. The city's job as an imperative connection in exchange networks becomes clear through the different cluster of relics recuperated from the seabed. Ceramics, gems, strict images, and coins uncovered during archeological unearthings act as unmistakable associations with the regular routines of Heracleion's occupants. The range of curios, including things of unfamiliar beginning, mirrors the city's situation as a center point for exchange and social trade, impacting the material culture of the district.

The investigation of Heracleion's lowered fortunes has provoked a reconsideration of old marine and navigational mastery. The city's area along the Nile Delta and its sea associations required a complex comprehension of route, shipbuilding, and exchange planned operations. The investigation of wrecks and harbor structures gives important experiences into the innovative headways that worked with sea exercises during Heracleion's prime. The lowered remainders of vessels and port offices add to how we might interpret antiquated sea advancements and the difficulties looked via sailors in the powerful waters of the Mediterranean.

While Heracleion's verifiable importance is irrefutable, the conditions encompassing its downfall stay a subject of progressing exploration and hypothesis. Speculations going from cataclysmic events, for example, tremors and rising ocean levels, to human-initiated factors, including subsidence and sedimentation, are being investigated. The investigation of silt layers and center examples plans to reproduce the ecological circumstances that prompted Heracleion's submergence, giving an extensive comprehension of the powers at play.

The difficulties presented by the investigation and conservation of Heracleion's lowered legacy are perplexing and complex. The sensitive idea of submerged conditions requests particular ways to deal with unearthing, preservation, and documentation. The coordinated effort between archeologists, sea life researchers, and protectionists is critical to guarantee the dependable and practical investigation of the site. Preservation endeavors center around balancing out and safeguarding recuperated antiquities to forestall quick weakening once presented to air and daylight.

The rediscovery of Heracleion and the continuous investigation of its lowered fortunes additionally convey suggestions for contemporary conversations about environmental change and the weakness of seaside urban communities. While Heracleion's submergence is credited to a blend of regular and anthropogenic variables, the equals with present day worries about rising ocean levels and beach front disintegration are obvious. The investigation of old seaside urban areas gives significant experiences into the drawn out elements of beach front scenes, accentuating the requirement for reasonable ways to deal with address the difficulties presented by ecological changes.

The divulging of Heracleion off the bank of Egypt embodies the groundbreaking job of innovation in submerged antiquarianism. High level marine study innovations, including sonar and attractive imaging, have changed the investigation of lowered destinations, empowering scientists to plan submerged landscapes with extraordinary accuracy. Remotely Worked Vehicles (ROVs) outfitted with cameras and sensors have worked with designated unearthings and constant perception of submerged scenes. The combination of innovation and human skill guarantees an extensive and nuanced comprehension of lowered legacy destinations.

Heracleion's rediscovery has dazzled the academic local area as well as resounded with the worldwide public, igniting interest in oceanic paleontology and the secrets that lie underneath the ocean. The charm of lowered urban communities and their secret fortunes addresses an all inclusive interest with the past and the untold stories that anticipate disclosure. As innovation proceeds to progress and our comprehension of submerged paleohistory develops, the investigation of lowered urban communities like Heracleion offers a door to the rich embroidery of mankind's set of experiences that lies underneath the waves.

The rediscovery and progressing investigation of the lowered city of Heracleion keep on disentangling layers of verifiable and social importance, giving a nuanced comprehension of old developments and their sea communications. As archeologists dig further into the secrets disguised underneath the waves, the lowered remains of Heracleion yield extra bits of knowledge that add to a more complete story of the city's past and its position in the more extensive embroidery of mankind's set of experiences.

One of the captivating parts of Heracleion's authentic importance lies in its association with old Egyptian folklore and the love of divinities. The city's devotion to Amun-Gereb, a huge god in the Egyptian pantheon, highlights its strict significance. The stupendous sanctuary devoted to Amun-Gereb, with its transcending sculptures and complicated carvings, gives an unmistakable connection to the profound practices and convictions that penetrated Heracleion's general public. The investigation of these strict designs not just reveals insight into the city's social and strict life yet additionally adds to the more extensive comprehension of how old Egyptians communicated their otherworldliness in seaside metropolitan focuses.

The archeological discoveries in Heracleion reach out past fantastic designs and strict antiquities to incorporate regular items that proposition looks into the day to day routines of its occupants. Earthenware, instruments, family things, and individual antiquities recuperated from the seabed give significant bits of knowledge into the material culture of the city. The variety of these curios, including those of unfamiliar beginning, confirms the cosmopolitan idea of Heracleion and the social trades that occurred inside its clamoring roads. The investigation of such commonplace yet fundamental things improves how we might interpret the social elements, financial exercises, and day to day customs of the city's inhabitants.

Heracleion's job as a flourishing port city is additionally highlighted by the investigation of its harbor offices and oceanic foundation. The leftovers of quays, docks, and trenches uncover the essential preparation and designing ability that described the city's way to deal with oceanic exchange. The design of the harbor mirrors a comprehension of flowing examples and navigational contemplations, underlining the city's dependence on its sea associations for financial flourishing. The investigation of these designs contributes not exclusively to the comprehension of Heracleion's oceanic exercises yet additionally to more extensive conversations about old marine advances and waterfront metropolitan preparation.

The cosmopolitan person of Heracleion turns out to be significantly more evident through the revelation of antiques with unfamiliar starting points. Imported products, like ceramics, amphorae, and statuettes, address the city's dynamic support in territorial and worldwide exchange organizations. The variety of social impacts appeared in these curios features Heracleion as a mixture where merchandise, thoughts, and imaginative styles united. The investigation of these unfamiliar curios not just improves how we might interpret Heracleion's financial ties yet in addition gives a preview of the more extensive social milieu of the Mediterranean during the city's prime.

The continuous investigation into Heracleion's destruction adds one more layer of intricacy to its authentic story. While cataclysmic events and natural elements are among the proposed causes, the interchange of human exercises, like land subsidence and sedimentation, can't be disregarded. The investigation of dregs layers and geographical arrangements encompassing Heracleion's remains adds to the recreation of the natural circumstances that prompted the city's submergence. This multidisciplinary approach, consolidating antiquarianism with topography and ecological science, improves how we might interpret the powerful powers that molded the destiny of waterfront urban areas in times long past.

Protection endeavors pointed toward safeguarding the lowered relics of Heracleion assume a critical part in guaranteeing the life span of these verifiable fortunes. The sensitive idea of curios recuperated from submerged conditions requires particular strategies to balance out and safeguard them once presented to air. Traditionalists utilize fastidious techniques, for example, electrolytic decrease for metal articles and freeze-drying for natural materials, to forestall quick decay. The progress of these preservation endeavors is central in defending Heracleion's lowered legacy for people in the future and empowering proceeded with research.

The investigation of Heracleion likewise reverberates with contemporary conversations about the effect of environmental change on waterfront locales. While Heracleion's submergence is accepted to have happened more than a thousand years prior, the equals with present day worries about rising ocean levels and ecological movements are undeniable. The investigation of old seaside urban areas gives important bits of knowledge into the drawn out elements of waterfront scenes and the versatile procedures utilized by old social orders.

The illustrations gained from Heracleion's destiny add to progressing discussions about the strength of beach front urban areas despite natural difficulties.

The worldwide meaning of Heracleion's rediscovery stretches out past insightful circles, catching the creative mind of the public around the world. The charm of lowered urban communities and their secret stories reverberates with an all inclusive interest before and the secrets that lie underneath the ocean. Heracleion's lowered fortunes have become images of the getting through ponders ready to be uncovered in the profundities of our planet's seas. The public's interest with the investigation of Heracleion mirrors an aggregate appreciation for the lavishness of mankind's set of experiences and the untold stories that keep on being uncovered through headways in submerged paleohistory.

The continuous experiences into the verifiable and social meaning of the rediscovered city of Heracleion extend our appreciation for the intricacies of old civilizations and their oceanic associations. The investigation of great designs, strict curios, regular items, and the cosmopolitan impacts implanted in Heracleion's lowered vestiges adds to an all encompassing comprehension of the city's past. The progressing multidisciplinary research, protection endeavors, and public commitment highlight the persevering through effect of Heracleion's rediscovery on the areas of antiquarianism, history, and natural science. As the investigation proceeds, the lowered city of Heracleion stays a signal, welcoming us to dig further into the secrets that lie underneath the waves and enhancing how we might interpret the interconnected embroidery of mankind's set of experiences.

Chapter 5

**The Mary Celeste
Ghost Ship Phenomenon**

The oceanic world has for some time been a performance center for baffling occasions, none maybe more confounding than the instance of the Mary Celeste, a phantom boat that entered the records of nautical history as a riddle that has resisted clarification for north of hundred years. The story of the Mary Celeste starts on December 5, 1872, when the boat was found untied in the Atlantic Sea, abandoned by its group, with no evident indications of battle or trouble. The conditions encompassing the Mary Celeste have filled hypothesis, paranoid fears, and a heap of speculations trying to unwind the secret of what happened on board the disastrous vessel.

The Mary Celeste, initially named the Amazon, was a 103-foot brigantine that had seen different proprietors and gone through a few name changes prior to winding up at the focal point of quite possibly of the most persevering through sea puzzle ever. On its last journey, the boat was directed by Chief Benjamin Spooner Briggs, an accomplished and very much respected sailor. The group incorporated Briggs' better half, Sarah, and their two-year-old girl, Sophia, alongside seven different mariners.

The spooky excursion of the Mary Celeste started in New York City, where it stacked a freight of modern liquor bound for Genoa, Italy. The boat set forth on November 7, 1872, under the order of Chief Briggs, leaving on what ought to have been a routine transoceanic intersection. Notwithstanding, destiny had different designs for the Mary Celeste and its team.

It was very nearly a month after the fact, on December 5, 1872, that the Canadian brigantine Dei Gratia detected the Mary Celeste uncontrolled around 400 miles east of the Azores. The group of the Dei Gratia was bewildered by seeing the apparently deserted vessel and chose to explore. After boarding the Mary Celeste, they were met with a creepy scene - the boat was without any trace of any indications of something going on under the surface, yet there were no signs of a battle or crisis. The boat's freight of liquor barrels was unblemished, and the group's very own effects, including assets, stayed undisturbed.

The secret developed when it became obvious that the raft was missing, despite the fact that the boat's log and navigational instruments were still ready. The sails were to some degree set, recommending that the boat had not been totally deserted carelessly. The weather conditions was accounted for as quiet and the ocean conditions great, further adding to the perplexity of the circumstance. The Mary Celeste showed up as though its group had disappeared immediately and inexplicably.

The revelation of the Mary Celeste in this exceptional state promptly ignited a rush of hypothesis and speculations endeavoring to make sense of the destiny of its group. One of the underlying hypotheses recommended injustice, with doubts of robbery or rebellion. Nonetheless, the shortfall of any indications of brutality or battle on the boat went against this speculation. The unblemished freight of significant modern liquor likewise made burglary an impossible rationale, as it would have been an enticing objective for crooks.

One more hypothesis proposed the chance of an assault by a monster ocean animal, like a goliath octopus or an ocean snake, driving the group to leave the boat in dread for their lives. In any case, marine specialists and scholars exposed this thought, refering to the absence of proof for such marine animals going after and crippling a whole group.

Cataclysmic events, like a waterspout or an unexpected submerged volcanic ejection, were additionally thought to be as possible reasons for the group's sudden takeoff. However, the weather conditions records and ocean conditions went against the probability of a disastrous occasion, as there were no reports of outrageous climate or seismic exercises nearby during the significant period.

Quite possibly of the most persevering through hypothesis recommended a breakdown or blast in the boat's freight. The modern liquor ready, which was exceptionally combustible, might have prompted a catastrophe that provoked the group to forsake transport. In any case, resulting examinations found no proof of harm to the freight barrels or indications of a blast.

The boat's siphons were ready to rock 'n roll, dispersing the thought of a disastrous occasion connected with the freight.

The subject of why the group would leave a stable vessel without evident reason became fundamental to the persevering through secret of the Mary Celeste. Speculations moved to the chance of a health related crisis, like an episode of sickness or harming, constraining the group to leave transport hurriedly. In any case, this hypothesis confronted difficulties also. The boat's log, which would almost certainly have contained insights concerning any medical problems or health related crises, was feeling the loss of its last passages. Without this critical record, the conditions prompting the team's flight stayed subtle.

The examination concerning the Mary Celeste went on with true requests and judicial procedures, yet none could give a conclusive solution to the secret. The actual boat, rescued and fixed, proceeded with its oceanic vocation under new possession, yet the haze of the unexplained occasions of December 1872 waited over its standing. The sea local area was passed on to wrestle with the persevering through riddle of the Mary Celeste, with different hypotheses and hypotheses competing for focus.

In the years that followed, the Mary Celeste turned into the subject of various articles, books, and, surprisingly, fictitious records that looked to wind around stories around the secret. Arthur Conan Doyle, the maker of Sherlock Holmes, composed a brief tale named "J. Habakuk Jephson's Assertion," which fictionalized the occasions encompassing the Mary Celeste and added components of interest and scheme.

The persevering through interest with the Mary Celeste can be credited to the conjunction of a few variables. The sheer unlikelihood of a whole team forsaking a secure vessel without abandoning obvious proof or documentation challenges customary comprehension. The shortfall of an indisputable clarification has energized the minds of scientists, history specialists, and lovers, prompting a huge number of speculations that keep on being discussed.

The Mary Celeste peculiarity likewise takes advantage of a more extensive human interest with the obscure and the puzzling. The immeasurability of the seas, with their profound and neglected profundities, has generally been a material for stories of sea secrets, ocean beasts, and phantom boats. The Mary Celeste, with its true riddle and absence of a delightful goal, encapsulates the charm of the unexplained that enamors the human mind.

Throughout the long term, different specialists and agents have returned to the Mary Celeste secret, utilizing current advancements and criminological procedures to reevaluate the accessible proof. In the late twentieth hundred years, a hypothesis arose recommending that the boat's freight of liquor could have delivered exhaust that, when joined with a particular arrangement of conditions, might have persuaded the team to think the boat was in unavoidable peril.

This hypothesis, known as the "vapor speculation," proposes that an apparent danger from the freight provoked the team to forsake transport hurriedly, abandoning the logbook and other documentation simultaneously.

While the vapor speculation offered a possible clarification, it didn't completely dissipate the secret. Pundits contended that the course of events and conditions expected for such a situation to unfurl were speculative and needed conclusive proof. Moreover, the subject of why the team would decide to take to a raft, leaving a safe vessel, stayed unanswered.

Lately, endeavors to disentangle the secret have consolidated progressions in innovation, including programmatic experiences, legal examination, and submerged antiquarianism. The point isn't just to comprehend the occasions prompting the

Mary Celeste's deserting yet additionally to uncover potential hints that might have been ignored or darkened over the progression of time.

The persevering through tradition of the Mary Celeste secret untruths in its verifiable importance as well as in its job as an image of the sea obscure. The story of the apparition transport keeps on catching the creative mind, motivating innumerable conversations, examinations, and imaginative translations. The shortfall of a conclusive goal guarantees that the Mary Celeste remains solidly secured in the domain of sea secrets, welcoming continuous investigation and hypothesis.

As innovation keeps on progressing, giving new instruments to examination and investigation, there stays the likelihood that the mysteries of the Mary Celeste may one day be uncovered. Whether through a leap forward in scientific science, a reevaluation of verifiable records, or the disclosure of recently ignored proof, the mission to unwind the secret perseveres. Up to that point, the Mary Celeste remains as a demonstration of the persevering through charm of sea puzzles and the everlasting interest with the secrets that lie underneath the outer layer of the world's seas.

The persevering through secret of the Mary Celeste keeps on enrapturing the minds of antiquarians, specialists, and devotees the same. As the years have passed, different speculations and theories have arisen, each endeavoring to reveal insight into the occasions encompassing the unwanted vessel. While the tale of the Mary Celeste is set apart by vulnerability and hypothesis, it likewise fills in as a window into the difficulties and vulnerabilities looked by mariners exploring the eccentric waters of the nineteenth century Atlantic.

One of the determined inquiries encompassing the Mary Celeste secret is the destiny of its team. The unexpected and apparently unexplained flight of Chief Briggs, his family, and the group stays at the core of the mystery. Without obvious proof or observer accounts, hypotheses flourish in regards to what might have constrained experienced mariners to leave a safe vessel.

Some have set that an unexpected and unforeseen crisis, maybe of an individual or clinical nature, provoked the team to take to the raft in a rushed endeavor to arrive at wellbeing.

The missing raft has been a point of convergence of hypothesis, as it is vital for figuring out the group's takeoff. The shortfall of the raft from the Mary Celeste filled hypotheses of treachery or a frantic getaway from an up and coming danger ready. However, the circumstances under which the raft was sent off and the purposes for its utilization stay tricky. Speculations including rebellion, robbery, or an assault by unfriendly elements have been to a great extent excused because of the absence of proof supporting such situations.

The boat's log, a significant report that might have given bits of knowledge into the occasions prompting the group's takeoff, was prominently missing its last passages. The shortfall of these records has been a critical deterrent in recreating the timetable of the Mary Celeste's last days adrift. Speculations in regards to think altering the log or deliberate exclusion of sections have been proposed, further obfuscating the waters of the secret. The absence of a reasonable story from the boat's log has considered a huge number of translations and hypotheses, adding to the getting through charm of the Mary Celeste secret.

The state of the Mary Celeste itself offered restricted hints with regards to what unfolded ready. The boat was tracked down in fit for sailing condition, with no obvious harm to its design or freight. The sails were set such that proposed a purposeful and controlled move as opposed to a turbulent or overreacted takeoff. The freight of modern liquor, an important product, stayed in salvageable shape, scattering speculations of burglary or burglary as a rationale in the team's relinquishment. The shortfall of indications of battle or misery on the boat's deck added to the perplexity of the circumstance.

Speculations connected with the boat's freight have been returned to with an end goal to comprehend the conditions prompting the group's flight. The freight of modern liquor, however undisturbed, has been viewed as an expected wellspring of risk. A few speculations propose that exhaust from the liquor, joined with explicit air conditions, might have made an apparent danger that drove the group to leave transport. This speculation, known as the "exhaust hypothesis," endeavors to make sense of the team's apparently hurried flight without abandoning obvious proof of an emergency.

Nonetheless, the exhaust hypothesis, in the same way as other others, faces difficulties and suspicion. Pundits contend that the circumstances expected for liquor exhaust to represent a danger to the team are speculative, and the shortfall of indisputable proof makes it challenging to validate this theory. The hypothesis likewise doesn't completely represent why the group would decide to take to a raft, leaving a fit for sailing vessel, in light of a freight related concern.

Lately, endeavors to unwind the Mary Celeste secret have consolidated progressions in innovation, including virtual experiences, legal examination, and submerged paleohistory. The point isn't just to comprehend the occasions prompting the Mary Celeste's deserting yet in addition to uncover potential hints that might have been ignored or darkened over the progression of time.

One road of examination has zeroed in on the boat's freight and the likely job of liquor exhaust in the team's takeoff. Virtual experiences and investigations have been led to investigate the believability of the vapor hypothesis. While these endeavors give important bits of knowledge, they likewise feature the intricacies of reproducing the specific circumstances that might have existed on the Mary Celeste quite a long time back. The absence of conclusive proof and the speculative idea of the exhaust hypothesis highlight the difficulties intrinsic in tackling a secret that has persevered for ages.

The persevering through tradition of the Mary Celeste secret untruths in its verifiable importance as well as in its job as an image of the sea obscure. The story of the phantom boat keeps on catching the creative mind, motivating innumerable conversations, examinations, and imaginative translations. The shortfall of a conclusive goal guarantees that the Mary Celeste remains immovably secured in the domain of sea secrets, welcoming continuous investigation and hypothesis.

As innovation keeps on progressing, giving new instruments to examination and investigation, there stays the likelihood that the privileged insights of the Mary Celeste may one day be uncovered. Whether through a leap forward in measurable science, a reevaluation of verifiable records, or the revelation of recently ignored proof, the mission to disentangle the secret perseveres. Up to that point, the Mary Celeste remains as a demonstration of the getting through charm of sea puzzlers and the timeless interest with the secrets that lie underneath the outer layer of the world's seas.

5.1 Examination of the eerie tale of the Mary Celeste, a seemingly abandoned ship found adrift at sea.

The scary story of the Mary Celeste, an apparently deserted transport viewed as uncontrolled adrift, has woven itself into the texture of oceanic legend, becoming perhaps of the most persevering through secret in nautical history. The story unfurls in the colder time of year of 1872, when transoceanic journeys were a typical and basic piece of worldwide oceanic exchange. The Mary Celeste, initially named the Amazon, left on a portentous excursion from New York to Genoa, Italy, weighed down with a freight of modern liquor. What happened during that disastrous journey, coming full circle in the revelation of the boat uncontrolled in the Atlantic Sea, has bewildered examiners, students of history, and fans for north of 100 years.

The vessel's name itself conveys a quality of secret and interest, as the Mary Celeste has become inseparable from the apparition transport peculiarity. The account starts with the boat's takeoff from New York on November 7, 1872, under the order of Skipper Benjamin Spooner Briggs, an accomplished and regarded sailor. Going with him were his significant other, Sarah, and their two-year-old girl, Sophia, alongside a team of seven mariners. The boat's freight of modern liquor, an important item, added monetary importance to the excursion.

Close to 30 days into the journey, on December 5, 1872, the Canadian brigantine Dei Gratia detected the Mary Celeste unfastened around 400 miles east of the Azores. The group of the Dei Gratia, drove by Commander David Morehouse, moved toward the strange vessel and made a surprising disclosure - the Mary Celeste was apparently abandoned. The sails were to some extent set, and the boat kept a similarity to arrange, however there was no indication of its group. The atmospheric conditions were quiet, and the ocean was serene, further developing the secret.

As the group of the Dei Gratia boarded the Mary Celeste, they were met with an uncanny sight. The boat gave off an impression of being in secure condition, with no apparent harm to its structure or poles. The freight of modern liquor, put away in barrels in the hold, stayed immaculate. The boat's log and navigational instruments were still ready, just like the group's very own effects, including resources. In any case, the raft was prominently missing, leaving a void in the vessel's supplement of fundamental gear.

The shortfall of the raft turned into a point of convergence of hypothesis and interest. It recommended that the team had left the boat purposefully however under conditions that stayed slippery. The deliberate condition of the boat, joined with the missing raft, filled a horde of speculations in regards to the destiny of the Mary Celeste's group. Hypotheses going from robbery and revolt to cataclysmic events and ocean beasts arose, each endeavoring to unwind the puzzle that covered the unwanted vessel.

The underlying hypotheses proposed the chance of injustice, with doubts of robbery or revolt on board the Mary Celeste. In any case, an exhaustive review of the boat uncovered no indications of viciousness or battle. The flawless freight of modern liquor, an important product, likewise went against speculations of burglary or robbery. The shortfall of any signs of a lawbreaker act brought up additional issues than replies, pushing specialists to investigate elective clarifications for the team's secretive flight.

One more hypothesis proposed the inclusion of ocean beasts or monster animals of the profound as the reason for the team's unexpected deserting of the Mary Celeste. Stories of tremendous ocean snakes and legendary animals tormenting the sea's profundities were pervasive in sea fables. Notwithstanding, marine specialists and scholars excused these ideas, underlining the absence of logical proof for such animals truly hurting a team or vessel.

Catastrophic events, like a waterspout or an unexpected submerged volcanic emission, were likewise thought to be as expected foundations for the team's take-off. However, the weather conditions records and ocean conditions went against the probability of a disastrous occasion, as there were no reports of outrageous climate or seismic exercises nearby during the significant period. The shortfall of harm to the boat's construction and the flawless freight additionally tested the feasibility of this hypothesis.

Quite possibly of the most persevering through hypothesis zeroed in on the boat's freight of modern liquor as an expected wellspring of risk. The hypothesis recommended that exhaust from the liquor, joined with explicit barometrical circumstances, might have made an apparent danger that drove the group to hurriedly forsake transport. This speculation, known as the "vapor hypothesis," intended to make sense of the apparently sudden and unexplained flight of the group without abandoning obvious proof of an emergency.

Nonetheless, the exhaust hypothesis confronted difficulties and suspicion. Pundits contended that the circumstances expected for liquor exhaust to represent a danger to the group were speculative, and the shortfall of conclusive proof made it hard to prove this speculation. The hypothesis likewise didn't completely represent why the group would decide to take to a raft, leaving a secure vessel, in light of a freight related concern.

The examination concerning the Mary Celeste went on with true requests and official procedures, yet none could give a conclusive solution to the secret. The actual boat, rescued and fixed, proceeded with its sea profession under new proprietorship, yet the haze of the unexplained occasions of December 1872 waited over its standing. The oceanic local area was passed on to wrestle with the persevering through mystery of the Mary Celeste, with different hypotheses and hypotheses competing for focus.

In the years that followed, the Mary Celeste turned into the subject of various articles, books, and, surprisingly, fictitious records that looked to wind around stories around the secret. Arthur Conan Doyle, the maker of Sherlock Holmes, composed a brief tale named "J. Habakuk Jephson's Assertion," which fictionalized the occasions encompassing the Mary Celeste and added components of interest and connivance.

The persevering through interest with the Mary Celeste can be ascribed to the intersection of a few elements. The sheer unlikelihood of a whole team forsaking a stable vessel without abandoning obvious proof or documentation challenges regular comprehension. The shortfall of a convincing clarification has powered the minds of specialists, students of history, and lovers, prompting a huge number of hypotheses that keep on being discussed.

The Mary Celeste peculiarity likewise takes advantage of a more extensive human interest with the obscure and the strange.

The immensity of the seas, with their profound and neglected profundities, has generally been a material for stories of sea secrets, ocean beasts, and phantom boats. The Mary Celeste, with its genuine riddle and absence of a delightful goal, encapsulates the charm of the unexplained that dazzles the human mind.

Throughout the long term, different analysts and specialists have returned to the Mary Celeste secret, utilizing present day advancements and legal strategies to reconsider the accessible proof. In the late twentieth hundred years, a hypothesis arose proposing that the boat's freight of liquor could have created exhaust that, when joined with a particular arrangement of conditions, might have persuaded the team to think the boat was in impending peril. This hypothesis, known as the "exhaust speculation," hypothesizes that an apparent danger from the freight provoked the team to forsake transport hurriedly, abandoning the logbook and other documentation all the while.

While the vapor speculation offered a possible clarification, it didn't totally dissipate the secret. Pundits contended that the course of events and conditions expected for such a situation to unfurl were speculative and needed conclusive proof. Moreover, the subject of why the group would decide to take to a raft, leaving a secure vessel, stayed unanswered.

As of late, endeavors to unwind the secret have consolidated progressions in innovation, including programmatic experiences, scientific examination, and submerged antiquarianism. The point isn't just to comprehend the occasions prompting the Mary Celeste's surrender yet in addition to uncover potential signs that might have been ignored or darkened over the progression of time.

The persevering through tradition of the Mary Celeste secret falsehoods in its verifiable importance as well as in its job as an image of the oceanic unexplored world. The story of the apparition transport keeps on catching the creative mind, rousing incalculable conversations, examinations, and imaginative translations. The shortfall of a conclusive goal guarantees that the Mary Celeste remains solidly moored in the domain of oceanic secrets, welcoming continuous investigation and hypothesis.

As innovation keeps on progressing, giving new instruments to examination and investigation, there stays the likelihood that the mysteries of the Mary Celeste may one day be uncovered. Whether through a leap forward in scientific science, a reevaluation of verifiable records, or the revelation of recently disregarded proof, the mission to unwind the secret continues. Up to that point, the Mary Celeste remains as a demonstration of the getting through charm of sea conundrums and the timeless interest with the secrets that lie underneath the outer layer of the world's seas.

The spooky story of the Mary Celeste, an apparently deserted transport saw as unfastened adrift, entices us to dig further into the layers of secret that hide this oceanic conundrum. As we explore the unfamiliar waters of hypothesis and guess, the persevering through charm of the Mary Celeste lies in its verifiable importance as well as in its job as a demonstration of the intricacies and vulnerabilities of life adrift in the nineteenth hundred years.

The story of the Mary Celeste interlaces with the more extensive setting of overseas journeys during a period set apart by blossoming oceanic exchange and investigation. The actual idea of these excursions, with their inborn dangers and difficulties, makes way for a story that opposes regular comprehension. In the core of this sea show is Skipper Benjamin Spooner Briggs, a carefully prepared sailor whose standing added a layer of decency to the Mary Celeste's disastrous journey.

The boat's transformation from the Amazon to the Mary Celeste reverberations the exciting bends in the road of its sea fate. The adjustment of classification appears to be practically prophetic, as though the vessel played anticipated its possible part as the hero in one of the best secrets of the great oceans. The excursion from New York to Genoa, weighed down with barrels of modern liquor, was, basically, a microcosm of the worldwide oceanic exchange organization of the time. Little did Skipper Briggs and his group had at least some idea that their journey would come full circle in a riddle that would resound through the passageways of time.

The significant second shows up right then and there of December 5, 1872, when the Dei Gratia, another vessel exploring the huge territory of the Atlantic, coincidentally finds the Mary Celeste. The scene that unfurls as the group of the Dei Gratia loads up the apparently deserted transport is scratched in sea history. The Mary Celeste, with its sails somewhat set, presents a frightful scene - a boat without any trace of its human caretakers, an oceanic puzzler ready to be disentangled.

The shortfall of the raft turns into an unpleasant theme, an unanswered inquiry that reverberations as the decades progressed. The raft, that fundamental vessel of endurance, is obviously missing, abandoning a void that fills hypothesis and speculations. Maybe the Mary Celeste's group, confronted with an odd danger, had turned to this little specialty as their main method for get out. However, the inquiries continue - why the raft? Why leave a fit for sailing vessel for the vulnerabilities of the untamed ocean?

Speculations encompassing the Mary Celeste are just about as different as the sea flows that support its secret. The underlying doubts of treachery, robbery, or uprising give way to a horde of speculations, each endeavoring to open the privileged insights of the apparently abandoned vessel. Ocean beasts and legendary animals, the stuff of sea fables, momentarily dance on the edges of the account, just to be excused by the sane personalities of marine specialists and scientists.

The freight of modern liquor arises as a key member in the show, with speculations rotating around its capability to create risky exhaust that could have prompted a feeling of looming destruction among the group. The "vapor hypothesis" endeavors to legitimize the team's hurried takeoff, imagining a situation where the apparent danger from the freight drives them to leave transport. In any case, this hypothesis, in the same way as other others, experiences doubt and difficulties, featuring the slippery idea of a conclusive clarification for the Mary Celeste secret.

As the narrative of the Mary Celeste keeps on charming the creative mind, it rises above the domain of sea history and turns into a social standard. The conundrum of the neglected boat tracks down reverberation in writing, with writers like Arthur Conan Doyle winding around fictitious stories around its secret. The persevering through interest with the Mary Celeste addresses a general interest in the obscure, the unimaginable profundities of the ocean, and the secrets that lie underneath the surface.

In the domain of sea investigation and revelation, the Mary Celeste stays an image of the unknown regions of the sea, both physical and figurative. Its unwanted decks and quiet quarters become an illustration for the huge scopes of the ocean, holding privileged insights that escape human perception. The inquiries encompassing the Mary Celeste constrain us to defy the vulnerabilities of life adrift, the unconventionality of nature, and the versatility of the people who actually thought about exploring the waves.

The Mary Celeste, with its otherworldly presence in sea history, moves us to recognize the restrictions of our comprehension and embrace the cryptic idea of the ocean. It welcomes us to ponder the mental fortitude and persistence of the individuals who cruised its decks, standing up to the obscure with every whirlwind and peak of a wave. As we explore the flows of hypothesis and request, the tale of the Mary Celeste allures us to investigate the secrets of the ocean as well as the complexities of the human soul that considered cruising into the unexplored world.

5.2 Scientific investigations into the circumstances surrounding the crew's disappearance.

Logical examinations concerning the conditions encompassing the group's vanishing on board the Mary Celeste have added a layer of intricacy to the persevering through secret. As analysts and agents look to unwind the conundrum that covers this unwanted vessel, progressions in innovation, criminological examination, and interdisciplinary methodologies have come to the front. The journey for answers reaches out past verifiable records and speculative hypotheses, digging into the domains of sea life science, science, and brain research to examine the accessible proof and uncover stowed away insights.

One road of logical investigation centers around the boat's freight of modern liquor and the potential job it played in the group's vanishing.

Assumptions proposing that vapor from the liquor might have incited the team to leave transport have provoked logical investigations into the credibility of such situations. Programmatic experiences, examinations, and substance investigations have been utilized to reproduce the circumstances that might have prompted the age of unstable exhaust inside the Mary Celeste's hold.

The "exhaust speculation" places that the modern liquor, put away in wooden barrels, might have radiated fumes under unambiguous states of temperature, mugginess, and ventilation. Assuming that these fumes arrived at a focus inside the boat that was seen as a danger by the team, it could have set off their rushed flight. Scientists have looked to comprehend the synthetic cycles engaged with the breakdown of liquor and the potential for rage age, considering variables like temperature varieties during the journey.

While the vapor speculation offers a logical system for making sense of the team's flight, it isn't without its difficulties. Pundits contend that the circumstances expected for liquor vapor to arrive at hazardous levels are speculative, and the shortfall of conclusive proof inside the Mary Celeste convolutes the approval of this hypothesis. The complexities of reproducing verifiable circumstances, including the condition of the freight, ventilation designs, and ecological variables, present critical obstacles in laying out a definitive connection between the liquor freight and the team's vanishing.

Legal examination of the boat's design, freight hold, and individual possessions has been a point of convergence of logical examinations. Oceanic archeologists and criminological specialists have inspected the actual proof inside the Mary Celeste to gather bits of knowledge into the occasions prompting the group's unexpected flight. The condition of the boat's gear, sails, and generally safety has been investigated to discover whether outer variables, like an unexpected climate occasion or crash, might have constrained the team to leave transport.

One of the difficulties in directing scientific examination on the Mary Celeste lies in the progression of time and the changes the boat went through after its disclosure. The rescue and ensuing fixes to the vessel, alongside the mediations of resulting proprietors, have brought up issues about the credibility and honesty of the leftover proof. In any case, the careful assessment of the actual leftovers of the boat gives important information that adds to the general comprehension of the secret.

Submerged paleontology plays had a significant impact in uncovering lowered hints inside the Mary Celeste. Jumping undertakings to the site where the boat was found have tried to archive the vessel's condition on the sea depths. High-goal imaging and planning advancements have permitted analysts to make definite three-layered reproductions of the boat, helping with the distinguishing proof of expected indications of harm or underlying issues that might have affected the team's choice to leave transport.

The assessment of the raft, or the deficiency in that department, stays a critical part of scientific examination. Understanding the reason why the team decided to involve the raft as their method for get out, abandoning a safe vessel, is vital to disentangling the secret. The shortfall of the raft has provoked investigations into its likely condition at takeoff time, whether it was stable, and in the event that its utilization was a determined choice or a frantic attempt.

Mental profiling and social examination have been integrated into logical examinations to investigate the human parts of the Mary Celeste secret. Clinicians and specialists in human way of behaving have examined the expected stressors and mental variables that might have affected the group's activities. The disengagement of being adrift for a lengthy period, joined with the vulnerabilities of nineteenth century oceanic life, may have added to an increased condition of tension or suspicion among the group.

The mental aspect additionally envelops the possible effect of social and cultural convictions on the understanding of seen dangers. Mariners of the time were knowledgeable in sea strange notions and the rich woven artwork of nautical old stories. The impact of these convictions on the group's view of their circumstance, particularly with regards to a new and possibly perilous freight, is a feature that researchers have investigated as they continued looking for a thorough clarification.

Hypothetical models from the field of human variables and ergonomics have been applied to comprehend dynamic cycles under pressure. Speculations, for example, the "instinctive" reaction and the effect of mental predispositions on insight have been considered to reveal insight into the psychological condition of the Mary Celeste's team. These interdisciplinary methodologies feature the diverse idea of the secret and the need to coordinate logical, verifiable, and mental points of view to develop a strong story.

The investigation of weather conditions and ocean conditions during the Mary Celeste's journey adds to the logical examination. Meteorologists and oceanographers examine verifiable climate information to perceive whether the vessel experienced uncommon or outrageous circumstances that might have set off the team's choice to leave transport. In any case, the accessible records from the nineteenth century present limits, and the exact weather patterns at the hour of the team's vanishing remain subjects of hypothesis.

Progressions in remote detecting advancements, including satellite symbolism and environment demonstrating, have given apparatuses to recreate past climate occasions with more noteworthy exactness. These devices permit scientists to recreate the barometrical circumstances the Mary Celeste might have experienced during its transoceanic intersection. The coordination of meteorological information into the logical request upgrades the relevant comprehension of the conditions encompassing the neglected vessel.

As logical examinations concerning the Mary Celeste secret advancement, interdisciplinary cooperation turns out to be progressively fundamental. The union of mastery from fields as different as science, prehistoric studies, brain research, and meteorology guarantees an all encompassing assessment of the accessible proof. While individual hypotheses and logical methodologies might offer fractional bits of knowledge, the combination of these viewpoints adds to a more nuanced comprehension of the situation that unfolded on board the Mary Celeste.

The innate difficulties in exploring a verifiable secret of this extent highlight the inborn intricacies of the sea world. The Mary Celeste, with its ghostly presence in nautical history, turns into a vessel for the transportation of freight as well as for the vehicle of human interest, logical request, and the unending mission for replies. As researchers wrestle with the puzzler of the unwanted boat, they explore the flows of vulnerability, looking to divulge the secret insights that lie underneath the outer layer of this persevering through sea secret.

The logical investigation of the Mary Celeste secret digs into unknown waters, exploring a complicated interaction of disciplines and strategies. As analysts endeavor to disentangle the conditions encompassing the group's vanishing, the conundrum of the neglected vessel uncovers the complex woven artwork of sea history, human brain science, and logical request.

Compound examinations of the freight hold, combined with trials and reenactments, look to translate the job of modern liquor in the team's strange takeoff. The exhaust speculation, suggesting that unpredictable fumes from the liquor set off the relinquishment, goes through thorough investigation. Scientists look at authentic circumstances, freight arrangements, and ecological factors to reproduce conceivable situations inside the bounds of the Mary Celeste. Notwithstanding, the test lies in accommodating speculative reproductions with the shortfall of substantial proof inside the authentic record.

Measurable investigation, both on and underneath the sea surface, gives a substantial association with the occasions of 1872. Oceanic archeologists carefully investigate the remaining parts of the Mary Celeste, sorting out a visual story of the boat's condition on the seabed. Cutting edge imaging advancements and submerged overviews add to reproducing the vessel's last minutes. However, the progression of time, rescue activities, and ensuing modifications bring up issues about the dependability and culmination of the criminological proof.

The shortfall of the raft stays a strong point of convergence in the examination, provoking inquiries concerning its condition and the group's reasoning for picking it for the purpose of departure. Logical investigation stretches out to the raft's possible stability, revealing insight into whether its nonappearance was a purposeful choice or a frantic demonstration. Social investigation and mental profiling become basic, investigating the team's psychological state and the impact of social convictions and odd notions on their insights.

Mental viewpoints acquaint a human aspect with the logical request, recognizing the psychological stressors intrinsic in oceanic life. The detachment, vulnerability, and possible neurosis of nineteenth century mariners become components to think about in figuring out the team's activities. The juncture of human variables, mental predispositions, and social impacts shapes a unique system inside which the Mary Celeste secret unfurls.

Meteorological examinations contribute significant experiences into the environmental circumstances the Mary Celeste could have experienced. Meteorologists and oceanographers break down authentic climate information, utilizing remote detecting innovations and environment displaying to reenact the transoceanic weather conditions. The mission to recognize whether the vessel confronted uncommon or outrageous weather patterns adds one more layer of intricacy, underscoring the requirement for a complete comprehension of the natural setting.

Interdisciplinary joint effort arises as a foundation of logical investigation into the Mary Celeste secret. The assembly of ability from science, prehistoric studies, brain research, and meteorology highlights the intricacy of the sea riddle. This cooperative methodology recognizes that the responses to the secret falsehood not inside the bounds of a solitary discipline but rather in the combination of different viewpoints.

The constraints of exploring a verifiable secret become obvious as specialists wrestle with inadequate records, changed proof, and the innate vulnerabilities of the nineteenth century sea world. The logical mission for answers turns into a unique course of revelation, exploring vulnerabilities and facing the difficulties of accommodating different strands of proof.

The Mary Celeste, with its unearthly presence in sea history, turns into a vessel for the vehicle of human request and the getting through journey for information. Logical examinations change the unwanted boat into a cauldron where verifiable riddles, human brain research, and innovative progressions unite. The puzzler of the Mary Celeste keeps on charming the minds of researchers, students of history, and fans, alluring them to wander further into the chasm of sea secrets, where the responses might lie concealed underneath the waves.

5.3 Theories and findings that shed light on the mysteries of the ghost ship phenomenon.

The phantom boat peculiarity, exemplified by mysterious vessels like the Mary Celeste, has powered a plenty of hypotheses and discoveries that look to enlighten the secrets that cover these neglected oceanic conundrums. As we dig into the profundities of hypothesis and investigation, the apparition transport peculiarity rises above the limits of oceanic history, wandering into the domains of brain research, odd notion, and the unfamiliar waters of the human creative mind.

Assumptions encompassing the apparition transport peculiarity range from the ordinary to the otherworldly, each endeavoring to interpret the incomprehensible conditions under which these vessels are viewed as afloat, apparently absent any trace of their human caretakers. One winning speculation recommends that ecological variables, like outrageous weather patterns or catastrophic events, may assume a part in the group's choice to forsake transport. The possibility that an unexpected and devastating occasion could drive mariners to take to rafts or leave transport quickly resounds with the intricacies of sea life.

In any case, the materialness of this hypothesis to each phantom boat experience is sketchy. While it might represent a few cases where vessels are found in trouble, it misses the mark in making sense of the shortfall of obvious indicators of battle or harm on specific deserted ships. The Mary Celeste, for instance, was found in fit for sailing condition, with no evident harm to its frame or apparatus. The division between the apparent danger provoking surrender and the absence of relating proof difficulties the comprehensiveness of natural elements as the sole clarification for the phantom boat peculiarity.

One more hypothesis that has caught the creative mind of students of history and lovers the same rotates around the likely job of robbery or crimes. The possibility that unfriendly powers could board a vessel, overwhelm its team, and hold onto control furnishes a story that lines up with the bold stories of the great oceans. However, a nearer assessment of phantom boats like the Mary Celeste uncovers a shortage of proof supporting the robbery speculation. The shortfall of indications of savagery, unblemished freight, and the secretive flight of the team without a battle overcome the traditional presumption related with sea robbery.

The otherworldly and paranormal parts of the phantom boat peculiarity add a layer of interest to the story. Stories of reviled vessels, tormented waters, and ghastly groups have penetrated oceanic legends for quite a long time. The thought that otherworldly powers could impact the destiny of a boat, driving its team to leave it in dread, takes advantage of a profound well of human interest with the unexplored world. While these extraordinary clarifications might give spellbinding stories, they remain solidly inside the domain of fantasy and legend, lacking exact proof or logical approval.

The mental cost of life adrift, combined with the disconnection and vulnerabilities of long journeys, brings a human component into the phantom boat secret. Speculations that dig into the psychological condition of the group, investigating the possible effect of pressure, suspicion, or dreams, offer a more nuanced viewpoint. The limits of a boat, the repetitiveness of the untamed ocean, and the mental difficulties inborn in sea life might add to a group's impression of dangers that lead to silly or frantic activities.

The Mary Celeste, specifically, has been exposed to mental examinations that consider the potential stressors looked by its group. The seclusion, combined with the vulnerabilities of nineteenth century sea life, turns into a mental setting against which the secret unfurls. The human brain, helpless to mental inclinations, may decipher harmless upgrades as dangers, prompting activities that resist sensible clarification.

The mental aspect presents a mind boggling transaction of variables that adds profundity to how we might interpret the phantom boat peculiarity.

Social and cultural impacts arise as huge contemplations in unraveling the secrets of the phantom boat peculiarity. Mariners of the past were saturated with sea strange notions, people convictions, and a rich embroidery of nautical legend. The impact of these social components on the translation of occasions adrift can't be disregarded. A team exploring through new waters or experiencing surprising peculiarities might credit powerful importance to their encounters, impacting their choices and activities.

The apparition transport peculiarity, with its blend of speculations and discoveries, highlights the multi-layered nature of sea secrets. While certain clarifications might line up with sane and exact points of view, others live in the domains of fantasy, legends, and the unexplained. The combination of natural, mental, and social elements makes a complicated mosaic that characterizes the phantom boat peculiarity as a rich and perplexing part of sea history.

Logical examinations concerning the apparition transport peculiarity expect to dissipate legends and give levelheaded clarifications to these sea secrets. Progressions in marine paleontology, scientific examination, and interdisciplinary methodologies add to disentangling the intricacies of deserted vessels. The assessment of wrecks, for example, the Mary Celeste, through submerged paleohistory offers a substantial association with the past, permitting specialists to examine actual proof and remake the occasions prompting relinquishment.

The phantom boat peculiarity, while dazzling in its secret, fills in as a sign of the difficulties and vulnerabilities looked by mariners since forever ago. As we investigate the hypotheses and discoveries that shed light on these sea riddles, we explore the waters of the past as well as the profundities of the human mind, social convictions, and the persevering through appeal of the unexplored world. The phantom boat, with its ghastly presence not too far off of sea history, keeps on coaxing us to investigate, question, and disentangle the secrets that lie underneath the outer layer of the world's seas.

The phantom boat peculiarity, with its heap hypotheses and discoveries, welcomes us to stand up to the intricacies of oceanic secrets that rise above customary comprehension. As we explore through the embroidery of hypotheses - from natural variables to heavenly impacts - the riddle of these unwanted vessels stays a consistently present sign of the vulnerabilities and difficulties looked by mariners over the entire course of time.

One convincing part of the apparition transport peculiarity is its capacity to catch the human creative mind. The narratives of deserted vessels uncontrolled on the untamed ocean, without any trace of their groups, summon a feeling of creepy interest. These sea conundrums become materials whereupon accounts of experience, misfortune, and the heavenly are painted.

The actual idea of the apparition transport peculiarity rises above the limits of authentic request, welcoming us to investigate the profundities of our aggregate mind and the getting through charm of the unexplored world.

Speculations that quality the deserting of vessels to ecological elements or catastrophic events give a reasonable system, lining up with the practical difficulties of life adrift. However, as we investigate explicit cases, for example, the Mary Celeste, errors arise that challenge the comprehensiveness of these clarifications. The shortfall of noticeable indications of battle, harm, or misery on specific apparition ships goes against the assumptions related with ecological dangers. The journey for experimental proof and logical approval becomes necessary to recognizing the conceivable and the speculative.

The entwining of mental components with the phantom boat peculiarity presents a human aspect that resounds with the intricacies of oceanic life. The detachment, dreariness, and vulnerabilities innate in lengthy ocean journeys make a mental setting against which the secrets unfurl. The group's psychological state, impacted by pressure, distrustfulness, or hallucinations, adds a layer of subtlety to the story. The investigation of the human mind turns into a fundamental part in understanding the reason why mariners could leave secure vessels, capitulating to unreasonable apprehensions or saw dangers.

Social and cultural impacts, implanted in oceanic notions and legends, further enhance the account of the apparition transport peculiarity. Mariners exploring new waters or experiencing strange peculiarities might decipher their encounters from the perspective of social convictions. The impact of these convictions on dynamic cycles, combined with the mental difficulties of sea life, adds to the intricacy of the secret. The phantom boat becomes a verifiable curio as well as a social image, mirroring the cooperative connection between marine networks and the baffling powers of the ocean.

Logical examinations, enveloping disciplines like marine prehistoric studies, measurable investigation, and meteorology, carry a thorough and observational way to deal with unwinding the secrets of the phantom boat peculiarity. The assessment of actual proof, submerged reviews, and headways in innovation offer an unmistakable association with the past. As specialists dig into the lowered remaining parts of phantom boats, they explore through layers of dregs and authentic records, looking to reproduce the occasions that prompted deserting.

The getting through interest with phantom boats lies in their capacity to rise above the limits of reality, spellbinding our minds and motivating a journey for understanding. Whether established in the items of common sense of ecological difficulties, the complexities of human brain research, or the rich embroidered artwork of social convictions, the phantom boat peculiarity stays a necessary piece of oceanic history. As we explore the oceans of hypothesis and investigation, the apparition transport allures us to uncover the insights that lie underneath the surface, helping us to remember the secrets that endure in the immense span of the world's seas.

Chapter 6

**Underwater Archaeology
Tools and Techniques**

Submerged paleontology remains at the convergence of science, history, and investigation, giving a door to disentangling the secrets concealed underneath the world's seas. As a specific part of paleohistory, it utilizes a different cluster of devices and strategies custom-made to the exceptional difficulties presented by lowered conditions. This multidisciplinary approach works with the investigation of wrecks as well as divulges depressed urban communities, old harbors, and an abundance of social legacy that lies underneath the waves.

One of the essential apparatuses utilized in submerged prehistoric studies is the remotely worked vehicle (ROV). These automated subs are outfitted with cameras, lights, and some of the time mechanical arms, permitting archeologists to investigate and archive submerged locales with accuracy. ROVs are fastened to the surface vessel, giving an ongoing video feed and control to scientists. This innovation has upset submerged investigation, empowering researchers to arrive at profundities that were once out of reach and catch high-goal pictures of lowered antiquities.

Related to ROVs, independent submerged vehicles (AUVs) assume a pivotal part in planning and reviewing submerged locales. AUVs are pre-customized and work autonomously of direct human control, following foreordained study ways and using sonar frameworks to make definite three-layered guides of the ocean bottom. These guides help archeologists in arranging unearthings and grasping the format of lowered structures.

The utilization of side-filter sonar is one more essential strategy in submerged antiquarianism. This innovation includes emanating sound waves that skip off the ocean bottom and submerged objects, making definite pictures of the geology and irregularities on the sea floor. Archeologists can distinguish likely destinations of premium through these sonar pictures, directing ensuing examinations.

Plunging stays a principal strategy in submerged paleohistory, permitting archeologists to lead active examinations and recuperate curios. Notwithstanding, making a plunge remote ocean conditions presents exceptional difficulties, requiring particular gear, for example, climatic jumping suits (Promotions). These suits give a controlled climate to jumpers, permitting them to work at incredible profundities for expanded periods while staying away from the dangers related with decompression.

Lately, progresses in marine advanced mechanics have presented the utilization of independent surface vehicles (ASVs) in submerged paleontology. These automated vessels can convey different detecting hardware, including sonar and magnetometers, to productively study enormous regions. ASVs add to the starter evaluation of submerged destinations and help in the distinguishing proof of expected focuses for additional examination.

Magnetometers assume an essential part in finding lowered archeological destinations, especially wrecks. Ferrous materials, like iron cannons or anchors, make attractive peculiarities that can be recognized by these instruments. By studying the ocean bottom with magnetometers, archeologists can distinguish regions with high attractive marks, giving important insights to the presence of metallic antiques underneath the waves.

The use of marine geophysics, including sub-base profiling and seismic reviews, upgrades the comprehension of the subsurface layers underneath the ocean bottom. Sub-base profilers utilize sound waves to enter the ocean bottom, uncovering the stratigraphy and potential archeological elements covered underneath the dregs. Seismic reviews include the utilization of acoustic signs to make cross-sectional pictures of the subsurface, helping with the ID of covered designs and curios.

Submerged uncovering is a sensitive and mind boggling process, requesting particular methods to guarantee the safeguarding of relics and archeological setting. Pressure driven pull gadgets, transports, and digs are utilized to eliminate dregs from removal regions cautiously. These devices permit archeologists to uncover and recuperate relics while limiting aggravation to the general climate.

The documentation of submerged archeological locales is a fastidious errand that includes itemized planning, photography, and photogrammetry. Photogrammetry, specifically, has turned into an important instrument for making exact three-layered models of lowered designs and curios. By consolidating covering photos taken from various points, scientists can recreate computerized models that offer exact estimations and an extensive comprehension of the site's format.

Protection of recuperated relics from submerged locales is a basic part of submerged paleohistory. The drenching of antiques in seawater for stretched out periods can prompt weakening brought about by erosion and natural action. To moderate these impacts, antiques are frequently treated with particular preservation strategies, like electrolytic decrease for metal items or synthetic adjustment for natural materials.

Archaeogenetics, a generally late expansion to the paleontologist's tool compartment, empowers the investigation of old DNA removed from submerged finds. This method can possibly give bits of knowledge into the human tenants of lowered locales, the types of creatures related with oceanic exercises, and the beginnings of materials utilized in development or exchange.

While submerged prehistoric studies has revealed wonderful disclosures, it faces various difficulties. The destructive impacts of seawater, the intricacies of remote ocean conditions, and the significant expenses related with submerged investigation present impressive impediments. Also, the moral contemplations of upsetting submerged graves and the requirement for worldwide participation in safeguarding lowered social legacy add layers of intricacy to the field.

The Antikythera Component, a mind boggling old Greek gadget found in a wreck off the shoreline of Antikythera, Greece, remains as a demonstration of the capability of submerged paleohistory. This cosmic instrument, trusted to trace all the way back to the second century BCE, exhibits the high level mechanical information on antiquated civilizations. The Antikythera Component features the significance of investigating lowered destinations in revealing mankind's mechanical and social legacy.

The continuous investigation of the Titanic, quite possibly of the most famous wreck ever, represents the nonstop headways in submerged prehistoric studies. The utilization of remotely worked vehicles, subs, and state of the art imaging innovation has permitted scientists to make nitty gritty guides of the Titanic's destruction and recuperate antiquities, adding to how we might interpret the boat's last minutes.

The appeal of submerged antiquarianism lies in the recuperation of antiquated curios as well as in the possibility to open the secrets of mankind's set of experiences concealed underneath the waves. The devices and procedures utilized in this field have developed essentially, extending the extent of investigation and empowering specialists to dig into lowered domains that were once distant.

As we explore through the profundities of the seas, investigating wrecks, indented urban areas, and lowered social legacy, the multidisciplinary idea of submerged prehistoric studies becomes clear, winding around together science, history, and innovation.

One of the most famous instances of submerged paleohistory is the revelation of the RMS Titanic's destruction. Arranged more than two miles underneath the outer layer of the North Atlantic, the Titanic's remaining parts have been a point of convergence for investigation since its disclosure in 1985. Submarines and remotely worked vehicles (ROVs) furnished with superior quality cameras play had a crucial impact in catching point by point pictures of the boat's design and relics dissipated across the sea depths. The utilization of state of the art imaging innovation, for example, photogrammetry, has permitted specialists to make many-sided 3D models of the site, offering a virtual window into the past.

Past wrecks, submerged antiquarianism stretches out its compass to old lowered urban communities. The depressed city of Heracleion, situated off the shoreline of Egypt, is a prominent model. Lowered for north of 1,000 years, this once-flourishing port city was found in the mid 2000s. Submerged archeologists, equipped with a blend of ROVs and jumping undertakings, have divulged great sculptures, complicatedly cut curios, and the remainders of an old civilization underneath the waters of the Mediterranean. The fastidious documentation and recuperation of these curios give important bits of knowledge into the regular routines, exchange organizations, and social acts of a former period.

In the domain of investigation apparatuses, independent submerged vehicles (AUVs) have become important resources. These automated vehicles, pre-modified for explicit overview missions, can cover enormous regions with accuracy. Outfitted with sonar frameworks, AUVs make itemized guides of the ocean bottom, recognizing possible archeological locales and directing resulting examinations. The proficiency and independence of AUVs make them fundamental devices for primer overviews and planning immense submerged scenes.

Submerged paleohistory uncovers actual curios as well as uses logical procedures to extricate important data from lowered conditions. Marine geophysics, incorporating techniques like sub-base profiling and seismic reviews, permits scientists to investigate the subsurface layers underneath the ocean bottom. By dissecting the reverberations and impressions of sound waves, archeologists gain experiences into the stratigraphy and potential archeological highlights covered underneath layers of residue.

Preservation of submerged curios presents an interesting arrangement of difficulties because of the destructive idea of seawater. Electrolytic decrease, a preservation technique utilized for metal items, includes applying a low voltage electrical flow to the curio. This interaction assists with diminishing the consumption and balance out the metal, protecting it for additional review. Traditionalists likewise wrestle with the sensitive undertaking of protecting natural materials, for example, wood or materials, through specific procedures that forestall decay upon openness to air.

While mechanical headways have enormously improved the capacities of submerged paleohistory, moral contemplations assume a vital part in directing the field. Upsetting submerged graves raises moral situations, requiring a harmony between logical request and regard for the sacredness of sea internment destinations. Worldwide coordinated effort becomes pivotal in exploring these moral difficulties, as lowered social legacy frequently ranges public limits, requiring collaboration for the safeguarding and investigation of these significant curios.

The difficulties and compensations of submerged paleohistory are maybe no place more apparent than in the investigation of the Antikythera wreck off the bank of Greece. Found in 1901, this old wreck yielded the Antikythera System, a complex outfitted gadget frequently alluded to as the world's most seasoned simple PC. Over a century after the fact, present day innovation, including ROVs and high level imaging gear, has permitted specialists to return to the site. The recuperation of extra antiques and the use of state of the art strategies, like DNA investigation, have revealed new insight into the boat's freight, team, and the more extensive setting of antiquated marine.

Submerged paleohistory isn't restricted to far off or old history; it likewise draws in with later sea legacy. The Second Great War wrecks, similar to the USS Indianapolis, act as submerged time cases, offering bits of knowledge into authentic occasions and the existences of the individuals who served. The revelation and investigation of these disaster areas contribute not exclusively to how we might interpret the past yet additionally to regarding the memory of the people who forfeited during seasons of contention.

As we explore the eventual fate of submerged paleontology, the joining of arising advances holds extraordinary commitment. Computerized reasoning (artificial intelligence) and AI calculations can aid the examination of tremendous datasets created during submerged overviews, robotizing the recognizable proof of expected archeological highlights. Furthermore, headways in mechanical technology and sensor advancements keep on refining the accuracy and proficiency of submerged investigation.

Submerged antiquarianism remains at the front line of logical request, authentic investigation, and mechanical development. The apparatuses and strategies utilized in this field have advanced to address the difficulties of lowered conditions, uncovering stowed away parts of mankind's set of experiences. From the investigation of notable wrecks to the disclosure of antiquated urban communities underneath the waves, submerged antiquarianism keeps on enrapturing our minds and reshape how we might interpret the past. As the excursion into the profundities of the seas unfurls, the apparatuses of investigation become instruments of logical disclosure as well as vessels that convey us into the lowered domains of our common legacy.

6.1 Overview of the specialized tools and technologies used in underwater archaeology.

Submerged paleohistory remains as a multidisciplinary field that spans the domains of history, science, and innovation, opening the mysteries concealed underneath the world's seas. The particular apparatuses and advancements utilized in this novel part of archaic exploration are vital to exploring the difficulties presented by lowered conditions, empowering analysts to investigate wrecks, depressed urban communities, and submerged social legacy. This exhaustive outline will dig into the different cluster of devices and advancements that characterize the scene of submerged antiquarianism.

At the front of submerged archeological investigation are remotely worked vehicles (ROVs). These automated submarines are outfitted with cutting edge camera frameworks, lights, and, now and again, mechanical arms. Fastened to the surface vessel, ROVs furnish archeologists with continuous control and a live video feed, taking into consideration exact route and documentation of submerged destinations. The development of ROV innovation has extended the compass of submerged archaic exploration to profundities that were once viewed as difficult to reach, giving extraordinary admittance to lowered curios.

Pair with ROVs, independent submerged vehicles (AUVs) assume an essential part in the looking over and planning of submerged locales. AUVs work autonomously of direct human control, following pre-customized ways to lead reviews of the ocean bottom. Outfitted with sonar frameworks, AUVs make nitty gritty three-layered maps, assisting archeologists with arranging unearthings and gain an extensive comprehension of the submerged scene. The effectiveness and independence of AUVs contribute altogether to the fundamental appraisal of possible archeological destinations.

Side-filter sonar innovation has turned into a foundation of submerged archeological studies. By emanating sound waves that skip off the ocean bottom and submerged objects, side-check sonar makes nitty gritty pictures of the geography and irregularities on the sea floor. These sonar pictures act as priceless devices for recognizing expected locales of premium, directing ensuing examinations, and uncovering the design of lowered structures. The reconciliation of side-filter sonar with different innovations improves the proficiency and precision of submerged archeological investigation.

Jumping stays a basic part of submerged paleohistory, permitting scientists to direct involved examinations and recuperate relics. In any case, the difficulties of making a plunge remote ocean conditions require particular hardware. Climatic jumping suits (Promotions) give a controlled climate to jumpers, permitting them to work at incredible profundities for broadened periods while keeping away from the dangers related with decompression.

Advertisements innovation upgrades the security and effectiveness of submerged unearthings, especially in testing and remote ocean conditions.

Marine geophysics, including sub-base profiling and seismic reviews, adds to the comprehension of the subsurface layers underneath the ocean bottom. Sub-base profilers utilize sound waves to infiltrate the ocean bottom, uncovering the stratigraphy and potential archeological highlights covered underneath dregs layers. Seismic studies include the utilization of acoustic signs to make cross-sectional pictures of the subsurface, helping with the recognizable proof of covered designs and antiques. These geophysical methods give vital experiences into the archeological capability of submerged destinations.

Magnetometers act as basic devices for finding lowered archeological destinations, especially wrecks. Ferrous materials, like iron guns or anchors, make attractive oddities that can be distinguished by these instruments. By studying the ocean bottom with magnetometers, archeologists can distinguish regions with high attractive marks, giving important insights to the presence of metallic antiquities underneath the waves. The mix of magnetometry with other study strategies upgrades the accuracy of site recognizable proof.

Submerged exhuming presents exceptional difficulties, requesting specific apparatuses to guarantee the cautious recuperation of antiquities and safeguarding of archeological setting. Pressure driven attractions gadgets, carriers, and digs are utilized to eliminate dregs from unearthing regions without causing unnecessary aggravation. These devices permit archeologists to uncover and recuperate antiques while limiting interruption to the general climate. Submerged uncovering procedures mean to safeguard the honesty of archeological locales and work with the careful recuperation of important social legacy.

Documentation of submerged archeological destinations is a fastidious undertaking that includes point by point planning, photography, and photogrammetry. Photogrammetry, specifically, has arisen as an amazing asset for making precise three-layered models of lowered designs and curios. By consolidating covering photos taken from various points, scientists can reproduce computerized models that offer exact estimations and a complete comprehension of the site's format. Documentation methods assume a significant part in safeguarding the archeological record and working with resulting examinations.

Preservation of recuperated curios from submerged destinations is a basic part of submerged paleontology. The submersion of curios in seawater for stretched out periods can prompt crumbling brought about by consumption and natural movement. To alleviate these impacts, curios go through specific protection techniques custom-made to their material structure. Electrolytic decrease, for instance, is utilized for metal items, including the controlled use of a low voltage electrical flow to lessen consumption and settle the metal. Preservationists likewise address the difficulties of safeguarding natural materials, like wood or materials, through cautious treatment and capacity.

Archaeogenetics, a generally late expansion to the prehistorian's tool compartment, includes the investigation of old DNA removed from submerged finds. This method holds the possibility to give bits of knowledge into the human tenants of lowered locales, the types of creatures related with oceanic exercises, and the starting points of materials utilized in development or exchange. Archaeogenetics adds to an all encompassing comprehension of submerged archeological locales by coordinating hereditary information with different types of proof.

While submerged paleontology has seen amazing disclosures, it faces various difficulties. The destructive impacts of seawater, the intricacies of remote ocean conditions, and the significant expenses related with submerged investigation present imposing deterrents. Moreover, moral contemplations of upsetting submerged graves and the requirement for worldwide collaboration in saving lowered social legacy add layers of intricacy to the field. Adjusting the quest for logical information with moral obligations is quite difficult for submerged archeologists.

The continuous investigation of notorious wrecks, for example, the RMS Titanic, epitomizes the nonstop progressions in submerged antiquarianism. The utilization of remotely worked vehicles, submarines, and state of the art imaging innovation has permitted analysts to make nitty gritty guides of the Titanic's destruction and recuperate ancient rarities, adding to how we might interpret the boat's last minutes. The investigation of lowered social legacy, going from old urban communities to The Second Great War wrecks, highlights the rich embroidered artwork of mankind's set of experiences ready to be divulged underneath the waves.

As innovation keeps on propelling, the fate of submerged antiquarianism holds extraordinary commitment. Computerized reasoning (artificial intelligence) and AI calculations can possibly aid the examination of immense datasets produced during submerged reviews, robotizing the distinguishing proof of likely archeological elements. The mix of arising innovations, mechanical technology, and sensor progressions keeps on refining the accuracy and effectiveness of submerged investigation, opening new outskirts in the mission to uncover lowered mysteries.

The particular devices and advancements utilized in submerged prehistoric studies address a captivating union of logical development, verifiable investigation, and mechanical ability. As we dig further into the complexities of this multidisciplinary field, it becomes apparent that these apparatuses are not only instruments however doors to opening the secrets disguised underneath the waves.

Remotely worked vehicles (ROVs) have arisen as crucial resources in the tool compartment of submerged archeologists. These automated subs, furnished with cutting edge imaging frameworks and frequently including mechanical arms, have reformed the investigation of submerged destinations. Fastened to surface vessels, ROVs give constant admittance to the profundities, permitting scientists to explore with accuracy and report lowered antiques in remarkable detail. The advancement of ROV innovation has extended the skylines of submerged antiquarianism, empowering researchers to arrive at profundities that were once viewed as past human access.

Independent submerged vehicles (AUVs) supplement the capacities of ROVs by offering a degree of independence in submerged reviews. These automated vehicles, customized for explicit review missions, explore foreordained ways to plan the ocean bottom effectively. Furnished with sonar frameworks, AUVs make nitty gritty three-layered maps, helping archeologists in arranging unearthings and figuring out the format of lowered structures. The collaboration among ROVs and AUVs has raised the effectiveness and precision of submerged archeological investigation.

Side-check sonar innovation assumes a crucial part in the underlying phases of submerged reviews. Transmitting sound waves that skip off the ocean bottom and submerged objects, side-examine sonar produces definite pictures of the sea floor's geology and oddities. These sonar pictures act as an aide for distinguishing possible locales of interest, empowering archeologists to come to informed conclusions about where to concentrate their endeavors. The joining of side-check sonar with different innovations improves the viability of archeological investigation by giving an extensive perspective on lowered scenes.

While state of the art innovation has extended the limits of submerged prehistoric studies, customary jumping stays an imperative part. Barometrical jumping suits (Promotions) have developed to address the difficulties of remote ocean conditions, offering jumpers a controlled climate to work at incredible profundities for broadened periods. Advertisements innovation improves security and productivity, permitting specialists to lead involved examinations and recuperate curios from testing submerged conditions. The marriage of trend setting innovation and conventional plunging skill guarantees an extensive way to deal with submerged uncovering.

Marine geophysics, including sub-base profiling and seismic overviews, gives a window into the subsurface layers underneath the ocean bottom. Sub-base profilers utilize sound waves to infiltrate the ocean bottom, uncovering the stratigraphy and potential archeological elements covered underneath dregs layers. Seismic studies, utilizing acoustic signs to make cross-sectional pictures of the subsurface, add to the recognizable proof of covered designs and antiquities. These geophysical methods offer important experiences into the archeological capability of submerged destinations, directing resulting removal endeavors.

Magnetometers arise as pivotal devices in the quest for lowered archeological destinations, especially wrecks. These instruments identify attractive peculiarities made by ferrous materials like iron guns or anchors. By reviewing the ocean bottom with magnetometers, archeologists can distinguish regions with high attractive marks, giving significant insights to the presence of metallic curios underneath the waves. The joining of magnetometry with other review strategies upgrades the accuracy of site recognizable proof, helping specialists in centering their investigation endeavors.

Submerged uncovering requests particular devices to guarantee the cautious recuperation of ancient rarities and the safeguarding of archeological setting. Pressure driven pull gadgets, transports, and digs are utilized to eliminate residue from removal regions without causing unjustifiable unsettling influence. These apparatuses permit archeologists to uncover and recuperate relics while limiting interruption to the general climate. The fragile idea of submerged unearthing accentuates the significance of saving the uprightness of archeological destinations and working with the fastidious recuperation of important social legacy.

Documentation of submerged archeological destinations is a fastidious cycle including itemized planning, photography, and photogrammetry. Photogrammetry, an incredible asset in this specific situation, makes precise three-layered models of lowered designs and relics. By consolidating covering photos taken from various points, scientists can remake computerized models that offer exact estimations and a thorough comprehension of the site's format. Documentation methods are fundamental to protecting the archeological record and working with resulting examinations.

The preservation of recuperated curios from submerged locales is a basic part of submerged prehistoric studies. Submerged in seawater for broadened periods, ancient rarities are vulnerable to decay brought about by erosion and natural action. Specific protection techniques are utilized, like electrolytic decrease for metal items. This interaction includes the controlled use of a low-voltage electrical flow to decrease consumption and balance out the metal, saving it for additional review. Progressives likewise address the difficulties of safeguarding natural materials, like wood or materials, through cautious treatment and capacity.

Archaeogenetics, a moderately ongoing expansion to the classicist's tool stash, includes the investigation of old DNA removed from submerged finds. This method holds the possibility to give bits of knowledge into the human tenants of lowered locales, the types of creatures related with sea exercises, and the starting points of materials utilized in development or exchange. Archaeogenetics adds to an all encompassing comprehension of submerged archeological destinations by coordinating hereditary information with different types of proof.

The difficulties looked by submerged prehistoric studies are diverse, from the destructive impacts of seawater to the intricacies of remote ocean conditions and the significant expenses related with submerged investigation. Moral contemplations encompassing the aggravation of submerged graves and the requirement for worldwide collaboration in protecting lowered social legacy add layers of intricacy to the field. Finding some kind of harmony between logical request and moral obligations stays a ceaseless test for submerged archeologists.

The continuous investigation of notable wrecks, for example, the RMS Titanic, epitomizes the persistent headways in submerged archaic exploration. The utilization of remotely worked vehicles, subs, and state of the art imaging innovation has permitted specialists to make point by point guides of the Titanic's destruction and recuperate ancient rarities, adding to how we might interpret the boat's last minutes.

The investigation of lowered social legacy, going from antiquated urban communities to The Second Great War wrecks, highlights the rich embroidery of mankind's set of experiences ready to be divulged underneath the waves.

As innovation keeps on propelling, the eventual fate of submerged antiquarianism holds extraordinary commitment. Man-made consciousness (artificial intelligence) and AI calculations can possibly aid the examination of tremendous datasets created during submerged studies, computerizing the recognizable proof of expected archeological elements. The joining of arising advancements, mechanical technology, and sensor progressions keeps on refining the accuracy and productivity of submerged investigation, opening new outskirts in the mission to reveal lowered mysteries.

The specific devices and advances utilized in submerged paleontology comprise a refined munititions stockpile that enables specialists to investigate the profundities of our sea past. From the utilization of remotely worked vehicles and independent submerged vehicles to cutting edge imaging procedures, these devices empower the fastidious investigation of wrecks, antiquated urban areas, and social legacy concealed underneath the world's seas. As we explore through the difficulties and compensations of submerged archeological investigation, the combination of science, history, and innovation turns into a signal directing us into the lowered domains of mankind's set of experiences.

6.2 Highlighting successful maritime archaeological expeditions.

Effective oceanic archeological undertakings address the apex of cooperative endeavors, mechanical progressions, and verifiable request, disclosing the secret accounts of our sea past. These undertakings, going from the revelation of antiquated wrecks to the investigation of lowered urban communities, enlighten the intricacies and wins of submerged paleohistory. In this investigation of outstanding campaigns, we cross the oceans and seas, diving into the profundities to uncover the mysteries saved underneath the waves.

One wonderful campaign that enamored the world's consideration was the disclosure of the RMS Titanic. In 1985, a joint French-American undertaking, drove by Jean-Louis Michel and Robert Ballard, used the remote ocean sub Alvin and the remotely worked vehicle (ROV) Jason Jr. to find the notable wreck. Situated more than two miles underneath the outer layer of the North Atlantic, the Titanic had evaded disclosure for quite a long time. The campaign's prosperity denoted a turning point in submerged prehistoric studies, permitting specialists to investigate and record the destruction in exceptional detail.

The mechanical developments utilized during the Titanic endeavor set another norm for remote ocean investigation. The utilization of ROVs furnished with superior quality cameras empowered specialists to catch pictures of the boat's construction, antiquities, and the garbage field dissipated across the sea depths.

The utilization of state of the art imaging innovation, for example, photogrammetry, permitted researchers to make unpredictable 3D models of the site, offering a virtual window into the past. The Titanic endeavor not just developed how we might interpret the boat's last minutes yet in addition exhibited the capability of cutting edge innovation in unwinding sea secrets.

Moving past the domain of present day wrecks, the unearthing of the Antikythera wreck off the bank of Greece remains as a demonstration of the versatility and devotion of sea archeologists. Found in 1901 by wipe jumpers, the Antikythera wreck yielded the Antikythera System, a complex outfitted gadget accepted to be an old simple PC. In 2014, a multidisciplinary campaign, named the "Return to Antikythera," utilized trend setting innovations, including ROVs and high-goal imaging frameworks, to return to the site.

Driven by archeologists Brendan Foley and Theotokis Theodoulou, the undertaking uncovered extra relics as well as used cutting edge procedures, for example, DNA investigation to concentrate on the remaining parts of human skeletal material found at the site. The revelations shed new light on the freight, group, and the more extensive setting of antiquated marine. The Antikythera campaign represents the marriage of old style paleohistory with state of the art innovation, pushing the limits of what is feasible in the investigation of lowered social legacy.

An outstanding progress in the domain of old lowered urban communities is the disclosure of Heracleion, otherwise called Thonis. Arranged off the shore of Alexandria, Egypt, Heracleion was a flourishing port city that bafflingly vanished underneath the waters quite a long time back. In 2000, Franck Goddio, a French submerged paleologist, drove a group that used a mix of ROVs, digs, and submerged removal methods to uncover the lowered city's mysteries.

The campaign uncovered fantastic sculptures, unpredictably cut relics, and the leftovers of a complex old progress. The cautious documentation and recuperation of relics from Heracleion gave significant experiences into the city's set of experiences, exchange organizations, and social practices. The effective investigation of Heracleion features the significance of interdisciplinary methodologies in revealing the tales of lost urban areas underneath the waves.

In the domain of The Second Great War sea paleohistory, the disclosure of the USS Indianapolis remains as a strong section. The USS Indianapolis, a weighty cruiser that assumed a significant part in conveying parts of the nuclear bomb during the conflict, was sunk by a Japanese submarine in 1945. For a really long time, the area of the destruction stayed obscure. In 2017, a group drove by Microsoft prime supporter Paul Allen and under the direction of sea paleologist Robert Ballard, found the remaining parts of the USS Indianapolis in the Philippine Ocean.

Using the exploration vessel Petrel and ROVs, the endeavor archived the destruction and honored the mariners who lost their lives. The revelation gave conclusion to the groups of the team and added to how we might interpret the occasions encompassing the boat's sinking.

The effective ID of the USS Indianapolis epitomizes the force of current innovation in finding generally huge wrecks and celebrating the penances made during wartime.

The Dark Ocean Sea Antiquarianism Venture, drove by analysts from the College of Southampton, has essentially progressed how we might interpret old marine in the Dark Ocean locale. Sent off in 2015, the undertaking used state of the art advances, including ROVs and AUVs, to review the Dark Ocean's profundities and reveal a large number of old wrecks crossing different verifiable periods. The review uncovered strikingly very much saved wrecks, some going back more than a thousand years, offering a brief look into the different oceanic exercises that formed the locale's set of experiences.

The Dark Ocean Sea Antiquarianism Task exhibits the capability of innovation to change archeological review strategies. The utilization of AUVs, specifically, considered the efficient planning of enormous regions, furnishing scientists with an extensive outline of the Dark Ocean's submerged social legacy. The progress of this task highlights the significance of cooperative global endeavors in investigating and protecting the rich sea history of our planet.

The continuous investigation of the Franklin Endeavor, a nineteenth century journey for the Northwest Entry, addresses an adventure of constancy and mechanical development. Sir John Franklin's campaign, comprising of the HMS Erebus and HMS Dread, set forth in 1845 yet bafflingly vanished in the Icy. For more than 100 years, the destiny of the campaign stayed quite possibly of the best secret in oceanic history. In 2014 and 2016, the disaster areas of the HMS Erebus and HMS Dread were at last found in the cold waters of the Icy by the Canadian Icy Undertaking, a cooperation between Parks Canada, Inuit associations, and different accomplices.

Using a blend of sonar planning, remotely worked vehicles, and independent submerged vehicles, the endeavor found the disaster areas as well as reported the surprisingly very much saved state of the boats. Mechanical headways in marine paleontology, including 3D displaying and submerged imaging, permitted analysts to investigate the insides of the boats and recuperate curios. The Franklin Endeavor's investigation exhibits how steadiness, joint effort, and headways in innovation can open the privileged insights of authentic sea secrets.

The Bermuda 100 Test, sent off in 2017, planned to report and examine 100 wrecks in the waters encompassing Bermuda. Driven by Dr. Philippe Rouja and a group of archeologists, the venture utilized a mix of ROVs, specialized plunging, and archeological study strategies to investigate the different exhibit of wrecks in the district. The undertaking not just added to how we might interpret Bermuda's oceanic legacy yet additionally stressed the significance of proactive preservation and documentation even with possible dangers to submerged social legacy.

The Bermuda 100 Test epitomizes the meaning of local area association and public effort in sea antiquarianism. By drawing in with nearby networks and cultivating a feeling of responsibility, the undertaking not just accomplished its objective of reporting 100 wrecks yet in addition brought issues to light about the significance of protecting and celebrating sea history.

The investigation of oceanic archeological locales has shown to be an intriguing excursion, set apart by wins, challenges, and the steady quest for uncovering stowed away chronicles. Each effective endeavor not just adds to our aggregate comprehension of the past yet additionally features the inventiveness of current innovation and cooperative examination endeavors. As we dig further into the chronicles of oceanic prehistoric studies, a few remarkable endeavors stick out, exhibiting the variety of lowered locales and the strategies utilized to uncover their insider facts.

The mission to reveal the secrets of the Dark Ocean has been a convincing section in sea prehistoric studies. The Dark Ocean Sea Paleohistory Task, started in 2015, was a cooperative exertion including scientists from the College of Southampton. Using trend setting innovations, for example, ROVs and AUVs, the venture planned to review the Dark Ocean's profundities and investigate its rich sea history.

The result outperformed assumptions, uncovering a gold mine of strikingly very much safeguarded wrecks spreading over different verifiable periods.

What sets the Dark Ocean project separated isn't simply the amount however the nature of the revelations. The anoxic states of the Dark Ocean, without any trace of oxygen that causes natural rot, added to the extraordinary protection of the wrecks. A few vessels, going back north of 1,000 years, held unpredictable subtleties, offering a novel window into old nautical societies. The progress of the Dark Ocean Sea Antiquarianism Undertaking highlights the capability of current innovation to upset how we might interpret lowered archeological scenes.

The Mediterranean, with its rich embroidery of civilizations and shipping lanes, has been a point of convergence for oceanic archeologists. The disclosure of the indented city of Heracleion off the shoreline of Egypt by Franck Goddio's group is a demonstration of the charm of lost urban communities underneath the waves. Heracleion, otherwise called Thonis, was a flourishing port city that bafflingly disappeared north of a thousand years prior. In 2000, the submerged paleohistory group set out on an aggressive undertaking, utilizing a blend of ROVs, digs, and exhuming methods to uncover the lowered mysteries of this old city.

The disclosures at Heracleion were completely staggering — titanic sculptures, unpredictable relics, and remainders of a clamoring human progress lay secret underneath the seabed. The fastidious unearthing and documentation endeavors gave a nuanced comprehension of the city's set of experiences, its part in oceanic exchange, and the social collaborations that molded its character. The outcome of the Heracleion endeavor features the meaning of interdisciplinary methodologies in sorting out the accounts of old lowered urban communities.

The continuous investigation of the Franklin Endeavor in the Icy addresses a victory of steadiness and mechanical progression. Sir John Franklin's doomed journey for the Northwest Entry in the nineteenth century became one of oceanic history's persevering through secrets. For a really long time, the destiny of the HMS Erebus and HMS Fear stayed obscure. In 2014 and 2016, the Canadian Icy Undertaking, drove by Parks Canada as a team with Inuit associations and different accomplices, at last found the disaster areas in the cold waters of the Icy.

The outcome of the Franklin Undertaking's investigation lies in the revelation of the disaster areas as well as in the mechanical developments that worked with itemized examinations. The utilization of sonar planning, ROVs, and independent submerged vehicles permitted analysts to record the astoundingly all around saved state of the boats and their insides. The recuperation of relics and the use of cutting edge imaging procedures added to a complete comprehension of the endeavor's lamentable story. The Franklin Campaign exhibits how present day innovation can unwind verifiable secrets covered in the frosty profundities.

In the domain of The Second Great War oceanic paleohistory, the revelation of the USS Indianapolis was a powerful snapshot of verifiable retribution. The weighty cruiser, scandalous for conveying parts of the nuclear bomb, was obliterated by a

Japanese submarine in 1945. For a really long time, the whereabouts of the USS Indianapolis stayed obscure. In 2017, a group drove by Microsoft prime supporter Paul Allen and sea classicist Robert Ballard found the destruction in the Philippine Ocean.

The effective recognizable proof of the USS Indianapolis not just given conclusion to the groups of the team yet in addition added to how we might interpret the occasions prompting its sinking. The campaign used trend setting innovation, including ROVs, to report the destruction and honor the mariners who lost their lives. The disclosure of the USS Indianapolis embodies how sea prehistoric studies can respect the memory of the individuals who served during wartime and enlighten the verifiable setting of urgent occasions.

The Bermuda 100 Test, initiated by Dr. Philippe Rouja and a group of archeologists, exhibited the significance of proactive preservation and documentation of submerged social legacy. Sent off in 2017, the venture planned to examine and report 100 wrecks in the waters encompassing Bermuda. Utilizing a blend of ROVs, specialized plunging, and archeological study strategies, the campaign accomplished its objective as well as connected with nearby networks to bring issues to light about oceanic history.

The Bermuda 100 Test epitomizes the meaning of local area contribution and public effort in sea prehistoric studies. By cultivating a feeling of shared legacy, the undertaking reported wrecks as well as stressed the significance of safeguarding and celebrating sea history. The progress of the Bermuda 100 Test highlights the job of cooperation and local area commitment in protecting submerged social legacy.

Fruitful sea archeological undertakings address the zenith of fastidious preparation, mechanical development, and a profound obligation to revealing lowered chronicles. From the profundities of the Dark Ocean to the cold waters of the Icy, these campaigns have pushed the limits of investigation and innovation, uncovering the narratives of old human advancements, wartime penances, and disastrous investigations. As we explore the oceans and seas, the accomplishments of sea prehistoric studies rouse a proceeded with mission for information and a significant appreciation for the secret fortunes that lie underneath the waves. Each effective endeavor enhances how we might interpret the past as well as allures us to investigate the strange domains of our oceanic legacy.

6.3 The role of interdisciplinary collaboration in uncovering and preserving maritime history.

The investigation and safeguarding of oceanic history comprise a multi-layered try that requests the combination of different disciplines, mastery, and systems. Interdisciplinary cooperation remains as a foundation in the journey to uncover, comprehend, and shield the lowered stories of our sea past. As we explore the mind boggling embroidered artwork of history disguised underneath the waves, the cooperative endeavors of archeologists, antiquarians, researchers, moderates, and neighborhood networks arise as essential parts in the safeguarding of our sea legacy.

At the crossing point of history and antiquarianism, the collaboration between these disciplines turns out to be especially obvious. Paleohistory, with its involved way to deal with revealing material culture, supplements authentic exploration by giving substantial proof of past oceanic exercises. The coordinated effort among archeologists and students of history empowers a more exhaustive translation of oceanic locales, wrecks, and lowered scenes. Through careful removal and documentation, archeologists expose the actual leftovers of oceanic history, while antiquarians contextualize these discoveries inside more extensive stories of nautical societies, shipping lanes, and maritime commitment.

The Dark Ocean Sea Paleohistory Undertaking epitomizes the force of interdisciplinary coordinated effort among archeologists and researchers. Sent off in 2015, the task expected to study the Dark Ocean's profundities and reveal an abundance of old wrecks. Driven by scientists from the College of Southampton, the group used trend setting innovations, including remotely worked vehicles (ROVs) and independent submerged vehicles (AUVs), to investigate the submerged social legacy of the district. The joint effort between oceanic archeologists and sea life researchers considered a methodical and mechanically progressed review of the Dark Ocean's profundities, uncovering a store of very much protected wrecks spreading over different verifiable periods.

The interdisciplinary idea of the Dark Ocean project stretched out past paleontology and sea life science to consolidate natural science. The anoxic states of the Dark Ocean, lacking oxygen that works with natural rot, assumed a significant part in safeguarding the lowered relics. Ecological researchers teamed up with archeologists to figure out the special states of the Dark Ocean and their effect on the safeguarding of wrecks. This cooperative methodology not just upgraded the logical comprehension of the district's environment yet in addition gave significant bits of knowledge into the safeguarding systems that add to the lavishness of submerged archeological destinations.

The effective joint effort among archeologists and researchers is additionally exemplified in the investigation of lowered scenes, where interdisciplinary examination reaches out to geophysics and submerged planning. By utilizing advances, for example, side-filter sonar and sub-base profilers, archeologists can make nitty gritty guides of the ocean bottom, uncovering stowed away designs and expected archeological locales. The joint effort with geophysicists and submerged study experts upgrades the accuracy and productivity of sea archeological investigation, permitting specialists to distinguish areas of premium for additional examination.

The submerged archeological investigation of antiquated lowered urban communities, like Heracleion off the shoreline of Egypt, exhibits the unique joint effort between archeologists, students of history, and designers. Driven by Franck Goddio, a French submerged paleontologist, the group used a mix of ROVs, digs, and removal strategies to uncover the privileged insights of this once-flourishing port city that disappeared more than a thousand years prior. The interdisciplinary cooperation took into consideration the cautious documentation and recuperation of great sculptures, relics, and engineering remains, giving a nuanced comprehension of the city's set of experiences, exchange organizations, and social practices.

The job of protectionists in oceanic prehistoric studies is foremost in guaranteeing the safeguarding of recuperated antiques. Interdisciplinary coordinated effort among archeologists and protection specialists becomes fundamental in tending to the remarkable difficulties presented by submerged unearthing. The submersion of antiques in seawater for stretched out periods can prompt crumbling brought about by consumption and organic action. Traditionalists utilize particular procedures, like electrolytic decrease for metal articles and cautious treatment for natural materials, to settle and safeguard the recuperated antiquities.

A prominent illustration of interdisciplinary cooperation in protection is clear in the safeguarding endeavors following the exhuming of the Mary Rose, a Tudor warship that sank off the shoreline of Britain in 1545. The Mary Rose project included a multidisciplinary group of archeologists, moderates, and researchers cooperating to recuperate and protect the boat's frame, weapons, and individual possessions of the team. The cooperation stretched out to the utilization of imaginative strategies, for example, freeze-drying for the boat's lumbers, to forestall rot and guarantee the drawn out conservation of the antiques. The outcome of the Mary Rose project features how coordinated effort across disciplines is fundamental in the disclosure as well as in the supported protection of sea archeological finds.

The interdisciplinary way to deal with sea history stretches out past the domain of actual antiquities to incorporate the investigation of old DNA, known as archaeogenetics. This arising field includes the cooperation among archeologists and geneticists to separate and investigate DNA from lowered skeletal remaining parts and curios. The investigation of old DNA gives experiences into the hereditary cosmetics of past populaces, their starting points, and their cooperations with oceanic conditions. Archaeogenetic research adds to a more all encompassing comprehension of oceanic history by incorporating hereditary information with archeological and verifiable proof.

The Mary Rose project, referenced prior, integrated archaeogenetic examination to concentrate on the remaining parts of the group individuals. By extricating DNA from the skeletal material, researchers had the option to acquire bits of knowledge into the lineage, wellbeing, and educational encounters of the people on board the Tudor warship. The cooperation among archeologists and geneticists extended the extent of request, revealing insight into the human parts of sea history and the different foundations of the people who cruised the oceans hundreds of years prior.

The interdisciplinary coordinated effort in oceanic history stretches out to the domain of social legacy the executives, where archeologists work intimately with government organizations, policymakers, and nearby networks to guarantee the capable investigation and assurance of submerged social locales. The security of lowered legacy includes legitimate systems, natural effect evaluations, and local area commitment to figure out some kind of harmony between logical request and moral obligations.

The UNESCO Show on the Security of the Submerged Social Legacy, took on in 2001, fills in as a worldwide legitimate system for the shielding of lowered social locales. Sea archeologists, teaming up with policymakers and lawful specialists, assume a critical part in pushing for the sanction and execution of such shows at public and global levels. Interdisciplinary coordinated effort in social legacy the board is essential in encouraging an aggregate obligation to protecting submerged archeological locales for people in the future.

The significance of local area association and coordinated effort with neighborhood partners is apparent in projects like the Bermuda 100 Test. Driven by Dr. Philippe Rouja and a group of archeologists, the undertaking planned to report and examine 100 wrecks in the waters encompassing Bermuda. The cooperative exertion included specialized plunging, ROV investigation, and archeological study techniques, displaying how interdisciplinary methodologies can add to the comprehension and protection of sea history.

The Bermuda 100 Test accomplished its objective of recording wrecks as well as underscored the job of local area commitment in sea archaic exploration. By including nearby networks and cultivating a feeling of pride over submerged social legacy, the task brought issues to light about the significance of saving and celebrating oceanic history.

The cooperation with nearby partners turns into an indispensable piece of moral and feasible oceanic prehistoric studies, guaranteeing that the advantages of investigation are shared and the social meaning of submerged destinations is regarded.

The investigation and conservation of oceanic history are characteristically connected to headways in innovation. The joint effort among archeologists and architects, especially in the improvement of submerged review and unearthing devices, upgrades the effectiveness and accuracy of sea archeological investigation. Remotely worked vehicles (ROVs), independent submerged vehicles (AUVs), and high level imaging advances assume critical parts in uncovering and recording lowered destinations.

The mechanical advancements in submerged archaic exploration are exemplified in projects like the Titanic endeavor. Driven by Jean-Louis Michel and Robert Ballard in 1985, the joint French-American endeavor used the remote ocean submarine Alvin and the ROV Jason Jr. to find and report the famous wreck. The coordinated effort between archeologists, architects, and remote ocean investigation experts worked with the investigation of the Titanic's destruction more than two miles underneath the outer layer of the North Atlantic. The utilization of cutting edge imaging innovation, for example, photogrammetry, empowered the production of point by point 3D models, adding to how we might interpret the boat's last minutes.

The combination of oceanic prehistoric studies and innovation is likewise apparent in the continuous investigation of the Franklin Endeavor. The revelation of the disaster areas of the HMS Erebus and HMS Fear in the Icy included the utilization of sonar planning, ROVs, and AUVs. The coordinated effort among archeologists and marine technologists considered the definite documentation of the strikingly very much protected state of the boats and the recuperation of antiquities. The mechanical progressions in marine prehistoric studies contribute not exclusively to the investigation of verifiable secrets yet additionally to the improvement of imaginative techniques for submerged overview and uncovering.

In the proceeding with account of oceanic investigation and protection, the job of interdisciplinary coordinated effort stays vital, winding around together the strings of history, science, innovation, and local area commitment. As we dive further into the mind boggling embroidery of lowered stories, the coordinated effort between different disciplines becomes a strategic need as well as a demonstration of the common obligation of uncovering and protecting our sea legacy.

One of the key convergences where interdisciplinary coordinated effort prospers is in the investigation of old wrecks and lowered relics. The cooperative energy among archeologists and history specialists considers a nuanced translation of these curios, putting them inside the more extensive setting of verifiable stories. This cooperative exertion turns out to be especially vital in understanding the social, financial, and international angles that molded oceanic exercises across various ages.

The Antikythera wreck, found off the shoreline of Greece, fills in as a strong illustration of the complex joint effort between archeologists, history specialists, and researchers. Found in 1901 by wipe jumpers, the site yielded the Antikythera System, an old simple PC. In 2014, the "Return to Antikythera" endeavor, drove by archeologists Brendan Foley and Theotokis Theodoulou, united specialists from different fields to return to the site.

Archeologists carefully revealed extra relics, while history specialists contextualized the finds inside the more extensive authentic account of antiquated marine and shipping lanes. Researchers contributed by applying state of the art advances, like DNA investigation, to concentrate on the remaining parts of human skeletal material found at the site. The cooperative endeavors not just enhanced how we might interpret the freight and group yet in addition showed the way that various disciplines can unite to uncover the diverse stories covered underneath the waves.

The mechanical component of interdisciplinary cooperation in oceanic investigation is exemplified by the headways in marine paleohistory. Remotely Worked Vehicles (ROVs), Independent Submerged Vehicles (AUVs), and high level imaging innovations have become basic devices, broadening the compass and accuracy of submerged investigation. The joint effort among archeologists and marine technologists in creating and using these advancements improves the effectiveness and extent of sea archeological undertakings.

The disclosure and investigation of the Titanic destruction in 1985 address a milestone accomplishment in this mechanical cooperation. The joint French-American endeavor, drove by Jean-Louis Michel and Robert Ballard, utilized the remote ocean submarine Alvin and the ROV Jason Jr. to explore the profundities of the North Atlantic. The marriage of paleohistory, remote ocean investigation, and innovation considered the definite documentation of the Titanic's remaining parts, giving bits of knowledge into its last minutes and starting a trend for resulting submerged undertakings.

In the continuous investigation of the Franklin Undertaking, innovation keeps on assuming a vital part. The utilization of sonar planning, ROVs, and AUVs empowered the revelation and nitty gritty documentation of the disaster areas of the HMS Erebus and HMS Dread in the Icy. The cooperative endeavors among archeologists and marine technologists exhibit how progressions in innovation contribute not exclusively to the disclosure of verifiable secrets yet in addition to the advancement of techniques in submerged review and exhuming.

Moderates, one more fundamental piece of interdisciplinary coordinated effort, are entrusted with saving the trustworthiness of recuperated antiquities. The drenching of antiquities in seawater presents remarkable difficulties, including erosion and organic rot. The joint effort among archeologists and preservation specialists includes utilizing specific procedures to settle and safeguard these antiquities for people in the future.

The Mary Rose project, based on the removal and protection of a Tudor warship, embodies the significance of interdisciplinary coordinated effort in curio preservation. Archeologists worked connected at the hip with traditionalists, using inventive methods, for example, freeze-drying to safeguard the boat's lumbers and forestall rot. The progress of the Mary Rose project highlighted how the cooperative endeavors of various disciplines are fundamental in the revelation as well as in the supported protection of oceanic archeological finds.

The interdisciplinary joint effort reaches out past the logical and mechanical domains to incorporate social legacy the board. Archeologists team up with policymakers, lawful specialists, and neighborhood networks to guarantee the mindful investigation and assurance of submerged social destinations. The turn of events and execution of legitimate structures, like the UNESCO Show on the Insurance of the Submerged Social Legacy, require the cooperative contribution of different disciplines to work out some kind of harmony between logical request and moral obligations.

The Bermuda 100 Test, with its accentuation on local area contribution and commitment, embodies the significance of interdisciplinary cooperation in social legacy the executives. Archeologists, policymakers, and neighborhood networks cooperated to explore and record wrecks in the waters encompassing Bermuda. The task accomplished its objective as well as brought issues to light about oceanic history and the need to safeguard submerged social legacy. The coordinated effort with neighborhood partners guarantees that oceanic paleontology isn't just a logical undertaking yet in addition a common obligation that regards the social meaning of lowered destinations.

The cooperative endeavors of archeologists, antiquarians, researchers, progressives, architects, policymakers, and nearby networks are the bedrock of effective sea investigation and protection. The interdisciplinary methodology unites assorted viewpoints, philosophies, and ability to unwind the secret accounts of our sea past. As we explore the oceans and seas, the combination of various disciplines turns into a compass directing us toward a more significant comprehension of our common legacy. Interdisciplinary coordinated effort not just uncovers the secrets hid underneath the waves yet additionally guarantees that the fortunes of our sea history are safeguarded, celebrated, and gave to people in the future.

Chapter 7

Preserving Our Submerged Heritage

Protecting our lowered legacy is an undertaking that rises above time and requires a fragile harmony between investigation, preservation, and dependable stewardship. The profundities of seas, oceans, and streams hold an abundance of archeological fortunes, going from old wrecks to lowered urban communities, each adding to how we might interpret mankind's set of experiences. As we set out on the excursion to uncover these secret accounts, the significance of saving these lowered destinations becomes vital to guarantee their social, verifiable, and logical importance perseveres for people in the future.

The conservation of lowered legacy starts with the cautious investigation and documentation of archeological locales. The cooperative endeavors of archeologists, students of history, and sea life researchers combine in the journey to uncover the mysteries hid underneath the waves. The submerged excavator's toolbox incorporates cutting edge innovations like Remotely Worked Vehicles (ROVs), Independent Submerged Vehicles (AUVs), and high-goal imaging frameworks. These apparatuses work with the revelation of lowered locales as well as empower nitty gritty planning and documentation without upsetting the fragile submerged conditions.

One of the noteworthy accomplishments in the investigation and safeguarding of lowered legacy is exemplified by the Dark Ocean Sea Archaic exploration Undertaking. Sent off in 2015, this cooperative exertion included specialists from the College of Southampton using state of the art advancements to overview the Dark Ocean's profundities. The Dark Ocean, with its anoxic circumstances protecting wrecks over centuries, turned into a mother lode of archeological disclosures. The efficient planning of antiquated wrecks traversing different authentic periods displayed the capability of trend setting innovations in revealing and saving lowered legacy.

Protection, with regards to submerged archaic exploration, stretches out past the actual relics to the environments that encompass these archeological destinations. The fragile equilibrium of submerged conditions requires a nuanced way to deal with investigation that limits unsettling influences. The joint effort among archeologists and sea life researchers guarantees that the techniques utilized in reporting lowered destinations think about the biological effect, safeguarding the ancient rarities as well as the encompassing marine life.

The conservation of lowered legacy isn't exclusively a logical pursuit; an aggregate liability includes social legacy the board and lawful systems. The UNESCO Show on the Security of the Submerged Social Legacy, embraced in 2001, remains as a milestone global legitimate instrument. It underlines the significance of defending submerged social legacy and urges joint effort between countries to guarantee capable investigation and insurance of lowered destinations.

Social legacy the executives includes the coordinated effort of archeologists, policymakers, lawful specialists, and neighborhood networks. The execution of legitimate structures, natural effect evaluations, and local area commitment are indispensable parts of mindful conservation. The joint effort with nearby partners guarantees that the investigation of lowered destinations is directed with deference for the social meaning of these conditions, cultivating a feeling of shared proprietorship and obligation.

The Bermuda 100 Test, sent off in 2017, is a demonstration of the significance of local area contribution in protecting lowered legacy. Driven by Dr. Philippe Rouja and a group of archeologists, the undertaking planned to examine and report 100 wrecks in the waters encompassing Bermuda. The cooperative exertion included specialized jumping, ROV investigation, and archeological review techniques. By drawing in with nearby networks, the venture recorded wrecks as well as brought issues to light about the oceanic history of Bermuda, imparting a feeling of satisfaction and obligation in saving their submerged social legacy.

Saving lowered legacy likewise involves the protection of recuperated relics. The submersion of ancient rarities in seawater for broadened periods presents exceptional difficulties, including erosion and natural rot.

The cooperation among archeologists and protection specialists becomes fundamental to guarantee the drawn out safeguarding of these antiques for people in the future.

The Mary Rose project, based on the exhuming and safeguarding of a Tudor warship that sank off the shoreline of Britain in 1545, exhibits the interdisciplinary coordinated effort in curio preservation. Archeologists worked intimately with moderates, using inventive strategies, for example, freeze-drying to protect the boat's woods and forestall rot. The progress of the Mary Rose project highlighted how coordinated effort across disciplines is fundamental in the disclosure as well as in the supported protection of sea archeological finds.

The preservation interaction is a fragile harmony between settling curios and keeping up with their honesty. Preservationists utilize particular methods customized to the material sythesis of every antique, whether it be metal, wood, or natural materials. The joint effort among archeologists and protection specialists guarantees that relics recuperated from lowered destinations are concentrated as well as saved in a condition that considers continuous examination and public presentation.

Public effort and schooling assume a significant part in the protection of lowered legacy. The joint effort among archeologists and instructors encourages a more profound comprehension and appreciation for sea history among the more extensive public. Through shows, instructive projects, and effort drives, the tales of lowered locales become open to a more extensive crowd, imparting a feeling of social pride and obligation.

The depressed city of Heracleion, found off the bank of Egypt, embodies the groundbreaking force of public commitment to protecting lowered legacy. Franck Goddio, the French submerged excavator driving the undertaking, teamed up with instructive foundations and social associations to impart the disclosures to people in general. Displays exhibiting antiques from Heracleion permitted individuals to associate with the lowered city's set of experiences and value the significance of protecting such locales for people in the future.

Protecting lowered legacy additionally includes tending to the difficulties presented by regular and human-prompted dangers. Environmental change, with its effect on ocean levels and submerged biological systems, represents a critical gamble to lowered archeological locales. The cooperation between archeologists, environment researchers, and earthy people becomes fundamental in creating methodologies to relieve these dangers and adjust protection endeavors to a changing submerged scene.

The investigation of the Franklin Campaign, a nineteenth century mission for the Northwest Section, features the difficulties presented by the cruel Icy climate. The disaster areas of the HMS Erebus and HMS Fear, found in 2014 and 2016, face the continuous danger of ecological factors like frosty temperatures, ice, and moving silt.

The joint effort among archeologists and environment researchers becomes vital in grasping the effect of these elements on the conservation of the disaster areas and creating techniques to shield them against future dangers.

Safeguarding lowered legacy isn't just about safeguarding curios and locales yet in addition about cultivating a practical way to deal with investigation. The cooperation among archeologists and policymakers includes supporting for dependable the travel industry and admittance to lowered destinations. Finding some kind of harmony between permitting community for instructive purposes and guaranteeing the drawn out protection of destinations requires cautious preparation and coordination.

The USS Arizona Commemoration in Pearl Harbor, Hawaii, remains as an impactful illustration of mindful safeguarding and free. The coordinated effort between archeologists, the Public Park Administration, and the U.S. Naval force guarantees that guests can honor the submerged ship while regarding the site's holiness. The USS Arizona Remembrance fills in as a sign of the penances made during The Second Great War and the significance of safeguarding lowered legacy with a feeling of worship and obligation.

Protecting lowered legacy is a continuous responsibility that requires the co-operation of people, establishments, and countries. The difficulties presented by the submerged climate, environmental change, and human exercises require a proactive and versatile way to deal with preservation. The UNESCO Show on the Security of the Submerged Social Legacy gives a structure to worldwide cooperation, stressing the common obligation of countries in shielding lowered locales.

Saving lowered legacy requires a nuanced comprehension of the difficulties and open doors intrinsic in investigating the profundities of our seas and oceans. The charm of oceanic secrets and the rich embroidered artwork of history disguised underneath the waves allure wayfarers, archeologists, and researchers to disentangle stories that have persevered through hundreds of years. Nonetheless, the protection of these lowered destinations requires a sensitive dance between logical investigation, preservation endeavors, and the basic to keep up with the biological equilibrium of submerged conditions.

One of the basic contemplations in protecting lowered legacy is the biological effect of archeological investigation. The joint effort among archeologists and sea life researchers becomes principal in guaranteeing that the strategies utilized in submerged unearthings and reviews are naturally capable. The delicate environments encompassing lowered locales, whether coral reefs, seagrass beds, or remote ocean natural surroundings, request cautious thought to limit aggravations during investigation.

Imaginative advancements, like ROVs and AUVs, have fundamentally improved the accuracy of submerged archeological investigation while moderating expected biological damage. The Dark Ocean Sea Prehistoric studies Task embodies this methodology, where specialists used cutting edge innovations to overview the Dark Ocean's profundities. By utilizing ROVs and AUVs, the venture limited actual associations with the submerged climate, considering definite planning and documentation without upsetting sensitive biological systems.

Conservation endeavors reach out past the prompt archeological site to include more extensive ecological contemplations. Rising worries about environmental change and its effect on ocean levels highlight the requirement for coordinated effort among archeologists and environment researchers. The potential dangers presented by environmental change to lowered locales, including expanded dis-integration and moving sedimentation designs, require a proactive way to deal with defending these destinations for people in the future.

The difficulties looked by the disaster areas of the Franklin Campaign in the Cold feature the significance of understanding and moderating the ecological effect. As environmental change advances rapidly in polar locales, the sensitive equilibrium of the Icy biological system is upset, influencing the safeguarding of submerged archeological destinations. The joint effort among archeologists and environment researchers is urgent in creating procedures to address these difficulties and guarantee the drawn out conservation of lowered legacy in the Cold.

Safeguarding lowered legacy is additionally inherently connected to the moral contemplations of archeological investigation. The joint effort between archeologists, policymakers, and neighborhood networks is fundamental in laying out rules and moral structures that offset the logical request with dependable stewardship. The UNESCO Show on the Insurance of the Submerged Social Legacy gives an establishment to global coordinated effort, underlining the moral obligation of countries to secure and safeguard lowered destinations.

The Bermuda 100 Test is a demonstration of the cooperative and moral way to deal with saving submerged social legacy. The venture planned to record wrecks as well as effectively drew in with nearby networks to bring issues to light about sea history. The joint effort among archeologists and nearby partners guaranteed that the investigation of lowered locales was directed with deference for social importance and moral contemplations, cultivating a feeling of shared liability.

A fundamental part of saving lowered legacy is public commitment and instruction. The cooperation among archeologists and teachers becomes instrumental in spreading information about oceanic history, paleontology, and the significance of protecting submerged social legacy. Presentations, instructive projects, and effort drives act as extensions between mainstream researchers and the more extensive public, encouraging an appreciation for our oceanic past.

The depressed city of Heracleion, found off the bank of Egypt, gives a commendable instance of the extraordinary force of public commitment to protecting lowered legacy. Franck Goddio's cooperation with instructive foundations and social associations worked with displays exhibiting antiques from Heracleion. These shows imparted the revelations to the general population as well as ingrained a feeling of satisfaction and obligation regarding safeguarding lowered legacy. Public commitment fills in as an impetus for cultivating an association among networks and the lowered locales that hold bits of their common history.

Protecting lowered legacy is a perplexing dance among investigation and preservation, requiring creative ways to deal with address the intricacies of the submerged climate. The reconciliation of innovation and preservation rehearses becomes fundamental in guaranteeing that the relics recuperated from lowered locales are concentrated as well as safeguarded for people in the future.

The Mary Rose project remains as a worldview of interdisciplinary coordinated effort in relic preservation. Archeologists, traditionalists, and researchers cooperated to foster imaginative procedures for protecting the Tudor warship's lumbers and forestalling rot. Freeze-drying, a strategy utilized in the protection cycle, considered the supported safeguarding of the Mary Rose curios, exhibiting how cooperation across disciplines adds to the drawn out preservation of sea archeological finds.

The mechanical headways in marine antiquarianism are instrumental in investigation as well as in creating supportable protection techniques. The continuous investigation of the Franklin Campaign depends on sonar planning, ROVs, and AUVs to record the disaster areas and recuperate relics. The cooperation among archeologists and marine technologists guarantees that these advances are applied in the revelation stage as well as in the preservation endeavors, improving our capacity to protect lowered legacy in testing conditions.

Protecting lowered legacy is an advancing undertaking that requires versatile procedures to address arising difficulties. The coordinated effort among archeologists and architects becomes essential in creating and carrying out advancements that can endure the afflictions of submerged conditions. Mechanical developments, like high level imaging frameworks and 3D demonstrating, contribute not exclusively to investigation yet in addition to the protection and documentation of lowered destinations.

The investigation of the Titanic destruction in 1985, drove by Jean-Louis Michel and Robert Ballard, displayed the joining of innovation in saving lowered legacy. The remote ocean submarine Alvin and the ROV Jason Jr. were utilized to explore the profundities of the North Atlantic, catching definite pictures and making 3D models of the notorious wreck. This cooperative exertion between archeologists, designers, and remote ocean investigation experts not just extended how we might interpret the Titanic's last minutes yet additionally added to the improvement of cutting edge imaging advancements in submerged antiquarianism.

Safeguarding lowered legacy is a dynamic and cooperative exertion that stretches out past individual undertakings to envelop a worldwide obligation. The interconnected idea of submerged conditions, archeological locales, and social accounts requests worldwide cooperation and shared assets. The cooperation between countries, as underscored by the UNESCO Show on the Insurance of the Submerged Social Legacy, fills in as a structure for capable investigation and protection.

Protecting lowered legacy is a diverse and cooperative undertaking that winds around together the strings of investigation, preservation, and moral stewardship. The coordinated effort between archeologists, antiquarians, researchers, traditionalists, policymakers, specialists, and neighborhood networks is the establishment whereupon the safeguarding of our sea past rests. As we explore the profundities of seas and oceans, the cooperative endeavors become a reference point directing us toward an economical and deferential way to deal with uncovering, monitoring, and praising the fortunes concealed underneath the waves. The protection of lowered legacy isn't just a logical pursuit; it is an aggregate liability to guarantee that the tales lowered in the profundities of our seas persevere for a long time into the future.

7.1 Discussion on the importance of preserving underwater cultural heritage.

The significance of safeguarding submerged social legacy rises above the domains of prehistoric studies and history; it stretches out to our aggregate character, comprehension of the past, and the obligation we bear toward people in the future. Lowered underneath the waters lie remainders of civic establishments, oceanic undertakings, and social trades that have formed mankind's set of experiences. The protection of submerged social legacy isn't just a logical basic yet a promise to shielding the different stories that structure the embroidery of our common legacy.

At the core of the conversation lies the acknowledgment that submerged social legacy is a non-inexhaustible asset. When lost or harmed, the relics, structures, and lowered scenes can't be reproduced or reestablished. These submerged locales are time cases, protecting crossroads in history with unrivaled validness. The disaster areas of old ships, the leftovers of lowered urban communities, and the curios laying on the sea floor are windows into the past, offering experiences into shipping lanes, marine advancements, and social trades that molded the course of civic establishments.

Safeguarding submerged social legacy is a fundamental part of keeping a thorough and precise verifiable record. While earthly paleohistory gives significant experiences into the existences of past social orders, submerged locales offer novel points of view on oceanic exercises, maritime engineering, and the interconnectedness of various districts. The disaster areas of boats, going from old vessels to maritime warships, act as stores of data about sea exchange, maritime fighting, and mechanical progressions that play played critical parts in molding mankind's set of experiences.

The Dark Ocean Sea Prehistoric studies Venture remains as a demonstration of the wealth of data protected in submerged destinations. The efficient overview of old wrecks in the Dark Ocean uncovered an assorted cluster of vessels traversing different verifiable periods. These disaster areas gave priceless experiences into the exchange organizations of antiquated civic establishments, the advancements utilized in transport development, and the monetary associations that prospered across sea courses.

Additionally, submerged social legacy adds to how we might interpret social variety and the interconnectedness of social orders. The curios recuperated from lowered destinations address the material parts of a culture as well as its immaterial legacy, including customs, convictions, and social practices. The indented city of Heracleion off the shore of Egypt, with its sculptures, sanctuaries, and engravings, fills in as a powerful sign of the social trades between old civilizations along the Mediterranean shipping lanes.

Safeguarding submerged social legacy additionally has significant ramifications for figuring out the effect of natural changes on past social orders. Lowered scenes, once presented because of ocean level vacillations, give proof of human settlements, land use examples, and variations to changing natural circumstances. The coordinated effort among archeologists and ecological researchers considers a comprehensive comprehension of how past social orders adapted to normal varieties and offers examples for contemporary difficulties connected with environmental change and ocean level ascent.

The meaning of safeguarding submerged social legacy isn't restricted to scholarly circles; it reaches out to the domain of training and public mindfulness. These lowered locales can possibly enrapture the minds of individuals around the world, cultivating an appreciation for history, archaic exploration, and the significance of ecological stewardship. Shows, narratives, and instructive projects based on submerged prehistoric studies act as incredible assets for drawing in general society and motivating a feeling of marvel and interest in our common past.

The revelation and investigation of the Titanic destruction, generally spread through different media, epitomize the public's interest with submerged social legacy. The cooperative endeavors of archeologists, researchers, and producers carried the tale of the Titanic to millions, starting interest in sea history and the secrets of the profound. Such open commitment not just adds to the enthusiasm for our social legacy yet in addition highlights the requirement for mindful investigation and conservation.

Protecting submerged social legacy is likewise complicatedly connected to the moral obligations of the worldwide local area. The UNESCO Show on the Security of the Submerged Social Legacy, embraced in 2001, addresses a coordinated work to lay out worldwide standards for the defending of lowered destinations. The show stresses the common obligation of countries to safeguard and save submerged social legacy and supports cooperation in tending to the difficulties presented by plundering, business abuse, and natural dangers.

The moral contemplations reach out to issues of proprietorship, bringing home, and the contribution of nearby networks. The coordinated effort among archeologists and partners, including native networks, neighborhood legislatures, and relative populaces, guarantees that the investigation and protection of submerged social legacy regard the privileges and viewpoints of those with a verifiable association with the locales. The Bermuda 100 Test, with its accentuation on local area contribution, embodies a cooperative methodology that esteems the contribution of neighborhood networks in the investigation and security of lowered destinations.

Saving submerged social legacy requests a sensitive harmony among investigation and protection. While the revelation of lowered locales is an interesting and significant undertaking, the strategies utilized should focus on the drawn out conservation of these destinations and their curios. The cooperative endeavors of archeologists and preservation specialists become fundamental in creating and executing methodologies to safeguard delicate materials from the destructive impacts of seawater and the natural difficulties of submerged conditions.

The Mary Rose project, zeroed in on the Tudor warship that sank off the bank of Britain in 1545, fills in as a worldview of the careful preservation endeavors expected in submerged paleontology. The cooperation between archeologists, traditionalists, and researchers brought about creative methods, for example, freeze-drying to safeguard the boat's woods and forestall rot. The outcome of the Mary Rose project highlights the significance of incorporating protection rehearses into the investigation and removal interaction to guarantee the supported conservation of submerged social legacy.

Saving submerged social legacy likewise includes tending to the difficulties presented by business abuse and unlawful plundering. The exchange submerged relics, driven by business interests, represents a critical danger to the trustworthiness of lowered locales. The cooperation between archeologists, policing, and global associations becomes fundamental in creating techniques to battle unlawful dealing and guarantee that submerged social legacy stays secured.

The difficulties are additionally compounded by progresses in innovation, empowering more noteworthy admittance to submerged locales for rescue activities. The fragile biological systems encompassing these destinations are helpless against aggravations brought about by unpredictable investigation and plundering. The cooperative endeavors of archeologists, policymakers, and tree huggers become urgent in supporting for mindful the travel industry and manageable admittance to lowered destinations, finding some kind of harmony between open commitment and the basic to safeguard these conditions.

Protecting submerged social legacy is indistinguishable from the more extensive talk on the worth of social legacy in cultivating a feeling of personality, congruity, and shared mankind. The accounts embodied in lowered locales talk not exclusively to explicit societies and social orders yet to the general human experience of investigation, exchange, struggle, and transformation to evolving conditions.

The cooperative investigation and conservation of these locales become a demonstration of our obligation to understanding, safeguarding, and praising the different social legacy that characterizes us.

Safeguarding submerged social legacy is a multi-layered try that includes exploring complex difficulties and embracing cooperative arrangements. The natural worth of these lowered locales lies in the verifiable experiences they give as well as in their ability to rouse, teach, and encourage a common feeling of mankind. As we dig further into the conversation on the significance of protection, it becomes obvious that the social, instructive, and moral components of this endeavor are interwoven, requiring an agreeable joint effort between different partners.

Socially, safeguarding submerged legacy is tied in with perceiving the meaning of different social articulations and the manners by which social orders have formed and been molded by their sea surroundings. The ancient rarities, structures, and lowered scenes are unmistakable signs of human inventiveness, imagination, and versatility. The cooperative investigation of these locales saves the material parts of societies as well as adds to the more extensive comprehension of human variety and the interconnectedness of civic establishments.

The submerged city of Heracleion, with its archeological fortunes found off the shore of Egypt, fills in as a powerful model. The cooperative endeavors of archeologists, jumpers, and social foundations disclosed a lowered city that was a center of exchange and social trade in the old Mediterranean. The sculptures, engravings, and compositional remainders give a brief look into the rich embroidery of Greek and Egyptian societies, displaying how cooperative investigation can enlighten the social interaction that characterizes our common legacy.

Instruction turns into a vital part of the conservation story, as it overcomes any issues between scholarly examination and public commitment. The cooperative endeavors among archeologists and teachers are instrumental in spreading information about submerged social legacy, archaic exploration, and the meaning of safeguarding these destinations for people in the future. Instructive drives, going from school projects to public displays, assume a significant part in imparting a feeling of interest and appreciation for our sea past.

The Titanic revelation, with its resulting public presentations and narratives, features the extraordinary force of cooperative instruction. The investigation drove by Jean-Louis Michel and Robert Ballard caught the world's creative mind and prodded revenue in oceanic history. Cooperative endeavors between archeologists, teachers, and news sources guarantee that the tales concealed underneath the waves contact a wide crowd, cultivating a persevering through association between general society and the fortunes of submerged social legacy.

Morally, the significance of safeguarding submerged social legacy is established in the standards of dependable stewardship, regard for social variety, and the acknowledgment of the freedoms of networks with authentic connections to these destinations.

The coordinated effort between archeologists, policymakers, and nearby networks is imperative in laying out moral rules that focus on the security of lowered destinations while regarding the points of view and interests of those straightforwardly impacted by these disclosures.

The UNESCO Show on the Security of the Submerged Social Legacy is a foundation in this moral structure, stressing the common obligation of countries in defending lowered destinations. The show supports joint effort and sets principles for the dependable investigation, assurance, and conservation of submerged social legacy. This cooperative exertion at the global level highlights the moral basic to safeguard these locales to serve present and people in the future.

Besides, the commitment with nearby networks in the investigation and safeguarding process is fundamental. The Bermuda 100 Test, which effectively elaborate nearby partners in the documentation of wrecks, fills in as a model for local area based coordinated effort. By incorporating neighborhood information, points of view, and worries into the safeguarding account, the cooperative endeavors guarantee that submerged social legacy is treated with the regard it merits, perceiving its importance to the character and legacy of networks.

Protection, as a basic part of conservation, requires cooperative endeavors to guarantee the supported security of lowered curios and locales. The joint effort among archeologists and preservation specialists includes creating and executing imaginative strategies to address the difficulties presented by the submerged climate. These strategies settle and safeguard antiques as well as add to the developing procedures of submerged preservation.

The Mary Rose project, with its emphasis on preserving a Tudor warship, embodies the perplexing cooperation expected in submerged protection. Archeologists and moderates worked connected at the hip to foster freeze-drying and other conservation techniques to defend the boat's lumbers. This cooperative methodology guarantees that the curios recuperated from submerged destinations are concentrated as well as protected in a condition that considers continuous exploration and public showcase.

Tending to the dangers presented by business double-dealing and illegal plundering requires cooperative endeavors between archeologists, policing, and worldwide associations. The exchange submerged relics compromises the uprightness of lowered locales as well as powers an unlawful market that takes advantage of our common social legacy. Cooperative drives that emphasis on observing, guideline, and bringing issues to light about the outcomes of stealing from assume an imperative part in fighting these dangers.

The moral contemplations stretch out to issues of proprietorship and bringing home, particularly when lowered destinations are related with native or relative networks. The joint effort among archeologists and partners guarantees that the investigation and conservation of submerged social legacy regard the freedoms and points of view of those with a verifiable association with the destinations. This cooperative methodology advances a more comprehensive and evenhanded comprehension of our common legacy.

As we explore the intricacies of safeguarding submerged social legacy, mechanical advancements become fundamental to improving investigation, preservation, and documentation endeavors. The joint effort among archeologists and designers works with the turn of events and use of trend setting innovations, like ROVs, AUVs, and high-goal imaging frameworks, which broaden the range and accuracy of submerged investigation.

The continuous investigation of the Franklin Endeavor, using sonar planning, ROVs, and AUVs, represents the coordination of innovation into the safeguarding story. These cooperative endeavors not just add to the revelation of authentic secrets yet additionally grandstand the job of mechanical progressions in extending the skylines of submerged paleontology. As innovation keeps on developing, cooperative endeavors will assume a vital part in tackling its true capacity for the more prominent comprehension and safeguarding of submerged social legacy.

7.2 Consideration of the environmental and ethical challenges associated with maritime archaeology.

The field of sea prehistoric studies, while offering an extraordinary window into our common mankind's set of experiences, wrestles with a heap of natural and moral difficulties that require cautious thought. As scientists, archeologists, and policymakers dig into the profundities of seas and oceans to reveal lowered social legacy, they should explore a complicated landscape that includes adjusting the quest for information with ecological manageability and moral obligations. In this investigation, we dig into the multi-layered difficulties related with sea pre-historic studies, analyzing both the ecological effect of submerged investigation and the moral contemplations that emerge chasing uncovering the mysteries concealed underneath the waves.

One of the premier ecological difficulties connected to oceanic antiquarianism originates from the expected aggravation of submerged environments during investigation and exhuming exercises. The fragile equilibrium of marine conditions can be upset by the actual presence of archeologists and the utilization of cutting edge innovations, like Remotely Worked Vehicles (ROVs) and Independent Submerged Vehicles (AUVs). The actual demonstration of examining wrecks or lowered destinations may accidentally prompt aggravations in the seabed, possibly affecting marine verdure.

Moderating these natural effects requires a smart methodology that coordinates joint effort between sea life researchers and archeologists. The Dark Ocean Sea Paleontology Task fills in as a striking illustration of such cooperation. The venture, zeroed in on deliberately looking over old wrecks, used cutting edge innovations to limit actual associations with the submerged climate. By utilizing ROVs and AUVs, analysts had the option to lead definite planning and documentation without upsetting the sensitive environments of the Dark Ocean.

The effect of environmental change adds an extra layer of intricacy to the natural difficulties looked by sea paleontology. Rising ocean levels, sea fermentation, and changes in water temperature can present dangers to lowered locales and ancient rarities. The Franklin Undertaking, a nineteenth century mission for the Northwest Section, features the weakness of submerged archeological destinations in polar districts. As the Cold encounters sped up environmental change, the disaster areas of the HMS Erebus and HMS Dread face continuous difficulties from frosty temperatures, ice cover, and moving silt.

Cooperation among archeologists and environment researchers becomes pivotal in understanding the ramifications of environmental change on submerged locales and creating methodologies for their safeguarding. The interdisciplinary methodology considers an all encompassing comprehension of what ecological elements mean for lowered social legacy and gives bits of knowledge into potential preservation measures.

Moral contemplations are fundamental to sea paleontology, especially concerning issues of possession, bringing home, and the inclusion of nearby networks. The investigation of submerged social legacy frequently converges with the authentic traditions of native and relative populaces, bringing up issues about the freedoms and viewpoints of these networks. The cooperative commitment with neighborhood partners is fundamental in guaranteeing that the investigation and safeguarding of lowered locales regard the social legacy and characters of those straightforwardly associated with these conditions.

The UNESCO Show on the Assurance of the Submerged Social Legacy, took on in 2001, highlights the moral obligations related with submerged paleohistory. The show underlines the requirement for cooperative endeavors, empowers regard for the social meaning of lowered destinations, and requires the contribution of neighborhood networks in dynamic cycles. This moral structure recognizes the assorted points of view on possession and legacy, perceiving the significance of inclusivity in the act of sea paleohistory.

The Bermuda 100 Test gives a down to earth illustration of moral joint effort in oceanic prehistoric studies. The venture, zeroed in on archiving wrecks in Bermuda, effectively drew in with neighborhood networks. By coordinating neighborhood information and viewpoints into the investigation cycle, the cooperative exertion guaranteed that the social meaning of the wrecks was perceived and regarded. This approach adds to moral practice as well as cultivates a feeling of shared liability regarding the protection of submerged social legacy.

The exchange submerged relics, driven by business interests, represents a huge moral test for sea prehistoric studies. The unlawful market for submerged social legacy can prompt the plundering of destinations, undermining their uprightness and denying the worldwide local area of important authentic experiences. The coordinated effort between archeologists, policing, and global associations becomes fundamental in creating procedures to battle unlawful dealing and guarantee that submerged social legacy stays secured.

The difficulties related with business abuse additionally stretch out to the possible contentions between the scholastic quest for information and the business interests of rescue activities. The revelation of wrecks or lowered destinations with important freight can make pressures between archeological safeguarding and monetary motivators. Finding some kind of harmony between these interests requires straightforward cooperation, moral rules, and a common obligation to focusing on the safeguarding of verifiable and social legacy over monetary benefit.

One more moral thought in sea archaic exploration is the mindful administration of recuperated ancient rarities. The joint effort among archeologists and protection specialists becomes essential in guaranteeing that curios are treated with the regard they merit and saved in a way that considers progressing examination and public presentation. The Mary Rose project, zeroed in on a Tudor warship that sank off the shoreline of Britain in 1545, represents the complicated coordinated effort expected in relic preservation.

The moral obligations stretch out to the scattering of information and public commitment. The cooperative endeavors among archeologists and teachers assume a crucial part in imparting the tales of lowered locales to the more extensive public. Instructive projects, shows, and effort drives add to the enthusiasm for sea history and the significance of protecting submerged social legacy. The Titanic revelation, with its ensuing public displays and narratives, represents how cooperative instruction can spellbind the public's creative mind and ingrain a feeling of marvel about our common sea past.

Saving submerged social legacy is firmly interlaced with the more extensive talk on ecological supportability. The fragile environments encompassing lowered destinations are powerless against aggravations brought about by investigation exercises, environmental change, and human effects. The cooperation among archeologists and natural researchers is fundamental in creating systems to relieve these dangers and adjust safeguarding endeavors to a changing submerged scene.

The conservation of the Franklin Endeavor wrecks in the Icy features the difficulties presented by the cruel polar climate. The continuous joint effort among archeologists and environment researchers includes observing the effect of ecological elements on the disaster areas and creating versatile systems to shield them against future dangers. This joint effort fills in as a model for tending to the ecological difficulties related with submerged paleohistory in delicate biological systems.

Mechanical developments likewise assume a significant part in tending to both natural and moral difficulties in oceanic paleontology. The utilization of cutting edge imaging frameworks, ROVs, and AUVs upgrades investigation and documentation as well as limits actual unsettling influences to submerged conditions. The joining of innovation into preservation rehearses guarantees that curios are saved in a way that limits natural effect and considers maintainable exploration.

The difficulties and contemplations illustrated highlight the requirement for an all encompassing and cooperative way to deal with sea paleohistory. Natural manageability, moral practice, and public commitment are interconnected angles that shape the direction of submerged investigation and conservation. The cooperation between archeologists, researchers, policymakers, nearby networks, and the general population becomes basic in exploring the mind boggling landscape of sea archaic exploration and guaranteeing that the fortunes concealed underneath the waves are protected for people in the future.

Ecological protection in sea antiquarianism reaches out past limiting actual aggravations to submerged biological systems. It additionally includes tending to the more extensive biological ramifications of archeological exercises. For example, the utilization of specific materials in unearthing and safeguarding cycles can have natural results. Cooperative endeavors among archeologists and ecological researchers are fundamental to guarantee that the materials and strategies utilized are naturally supportable.

The presentation of poisons into the submerged climate during uncovering represents a likely danger to marine life. Substances utilized in the protection of antiquities, like synthetic compounds or coatings, may significantly affect the encompassing biological system. In this manner, the cooperation among archeologists and ecological specialists becomes pivotal in recognizing harmless to the ecosystem safeguarding methods that limit mischief to submerged territories.

Moreover, the removal of waste produced during archeological activities, whether coastal or seaward, requires cautious thought. Cooperative drives ought to zero in on carrying out mindful waste administration practices to forestall the contamination of seas and beach front regions. This part of natural stewardship features the requirement for a comprehensive way to deal with oceanic paleohistory — one that investigates and saves lowered locales as well as protections the strength of the marine climate.

Environmental change further intensifies the natural difficulties looked by sea paleontology. The sped up speed of environmental change influences ocean levels, sea flows, and temperature, straightforwardly affecting the protection of submerged social legacy. As ocean levels rise, beach front and submerged destinations face expanded dangers from disintegration, loss of residue cover, and openness to additional extraordinary natural circumstances.

The cooperative endeavors of archeologists and environment researchers become central in creating versatile systems to alleviate the effect of environmental change on lowered destinations. Observing and demonstrating the impacts of ecological changes give significant bits of knowledge that illuminate protection endeavors. The Franklin Endeavor wrecks, arranged in the quickly changing Cold climate, represent the requirement for continuous coordinated effort to address the developing difficulties presented by environmental change.

Moral contemplations in oceanic antiquarianism reach out to issues of social awareness and the deferential treatment of human remaining parts. The disclosure of wrecks or submerged destinations with related human remaining parts adds a layer of intricacy to the moral obligations of archeologists. Cooperative commitment with relative networks, native gatherings, and applicable partners is fundamental to explore the moral intricacies encompassing human remaining parts and entombment destinations.

The H.L. Hunley, a Nationwide conflict submarine recuperated off the shoreline of South Carolina, epitomizes the moral difficulties related with human remaining parts in submerged paleohistory. The joint effort between archeologists, scientific specialists, and relative networks was vital in taking care of the sensitive moral contemplations encompassing the recuperation and investigation of the submarine's group. This cooperative methodology guarantees that the investigation of lowered locales is directed with social awareness and regard for the respect of the people who might have died.

Social responsiveness is additionally relevant while thinking about the commercialization of submerged social legacy. The charm of important curios from wrecks can prompt contentions between the scholastic quest for information and business interests. Cooperative endeavors between archeologists, policymakers, and industry partners are important to work out some kind of harmony between the safeguarding of authentic and social legacy and the potential monetary impetuses related with significant finds.

The moral obligations stretch out to the portrayal and understanding of lowered locales. Cooperative endeavors among archeologists and legacy translators guarantee that the accounts of submerged social legacy are imparted precisely and with social awareness. Public commitment drives, like historical centers, displays, and instructive projects, assume an imperative part in encouraging a nuanced comprehension of sea history and the significance of moral conservation rehearses.

The natural and moral difficulties related with oceanic prehistoric studies require a cooperative and interdisciplinary methodology. The investigation and protection of submerged social legacy request logical thoroughness as well as a promise to ecological supportability, social responsiveness, and capable stewardship. As we keep on unwinding the secrets concealed underneath the waves, the cooperative endeavors of archeologists, researchers, policymakers, neighborhood networks, and the public become basic to guaranteeing that our oceanic past is investigated, comprehended, and protected in a way that regards both the climate and the different social stories exemplified in lowered destinations.

7.3 Reflection on the ongoing efforts to safeguard and interpret the secrets hidden in the ocean depths.

The continuous undertakings to shield and decipher the mysteries disguised in the sea profundities address a complex and cooperative excursion, entwining logical investigation, preservation endeavors, social responsiveness, and public commitment. As we consider these continuous endeavors, it becomes clear that the secrets concealed underneath the waves are not only relics to be revealed yet accounts that interface us to our oceanic past, forming how we might interpret history, character, and the climate.

At the core of these continuous endeavors lies the obligation to capable investigation, a rule that highlights the fragile harmony between unwinding verifiable secrets and saving the uprightness of lowered destinations. The mechanical progressions in submerged antiquarianism, from Remotely Worked Vehicles (ROVs) to Independent Submerged Vehicles (AUVs), have extended our ability to investigate the sea profundities while limiting actual aggravations to sensitive biological systems. The cooperative combination of these innovations with conventional archeological techniques takes into consideration careful planning, documentation, and recovery of curios, all directed with a sharp consciousness of the ecological effect.

The Dark Ocean Sea Paleohistory Task remains as a demonstration of the outcome of mindful investigation. By using cutting edge innovations, including ROVs and AUVs, analysts had the option to study and record old wrecks in the Dark Ocean with uncommon accuracy. The joint effort among archeologists and sea life researchers in this venture represents the amicable harmony between logical request and natural stewardship, showing the way that the mysteries of the profound can be disclosed with negligible environmental effect.

Protection endeavors comprise a necessary piece of continuous drives, guaranteeing that the fortunes recuperated from submerged destinations are saved for people in the future. The coordinated effort among archeologists and preservation specialists includes creating imaginative procedures to shield delicate materials from the destructive impacts of seawater and the difficulties presented by the submerged climate. From the freeze-drying of Tudor warship lumbers in the Mary Rose task to the careful protection of the Franklin Campaign antiques, these cooperative undertakings exhibit the devotion to defending the actual remainders of our sea legacy.

Be that as it may, the protection endeavors reach out past the research facility to incorporate the more extensive moral contemplations related with submerged paleohistory. The dependable administration of human remaining parts, the treatment of antiques with social awareness, and the commitment with relative networks feature the diverse idea of preservation in oceanic antiquarianism.

The H.L. Hunley, a Nationwide conflict submarine recuperation, epitomizes the cooperative and moral way to deal with managing human remaining parts, perceiving the significance of social responsiveness and regard for the pride of the individuals who died.

Social responsiveness is an all-encompassing subject that penetrates progressing endeavors in oceanic prehistoric studies. The investigation and understanding of lowered destinations frequently cross with the traditions of native and relative networks, bringing up issues about possession, bringing home, and the depiction of social accounts. The cooperative commitment with neighborhood partners, as exemplified in the Bermuda 100 Test, underlines the significance of coordinating nearby information, points of view, and worries into the investigation and protection processes.

Besides, the continuous drives recognize the basic of comprehensive narrating. Cooperative endeavors among archeologists and legacy translators endeavor to impart the meaning of lowered locales precisely and with social awareness. The portrayal and translation of submerged social legacy, through historical centers, shows, and instructive projects, become fundamental in encouraging a nuanced comprehension of oceanic history that mirrors the variety of social stories exemplified in these secret fortunes.

Public commitment arises as a foundation in the continuous endeavors to decipher and share the mysteries concealed in the sea profundities. The interest with oceanic secrets, typified by the revelation of the Titanic destruction, highlights the public's getting through interest in our common sea past. Cooperative instructive projects, narratives, and shows act as integral assets to charm minds, ingrain a feeling of miracle, and convey the significance of protecting submerged social legacy. The crossing point between science correspondence and public commitment turns into a unique space where the continuous disclosures underneath the waves rise above scholastic circles, reverberating with a worldwide crowd.

The Titanic disclosure, a cooperative exertion drove by Jean-Louis Michel and Robert Ballard, denoted a turning point in open commitment with submerged social legacy. The resulting presentations, narratives, and far and wide media inclusion carried the tale of the Titanic to millions, cultivating an aggregate association with the secrets of the profound. This cooperative undertaking between archeologists, researchers, and news sources exhibits the groundbreaking force of public commitment, transforming lowered curios into social standards that rise above scholarly limits.

As we ponder the continuous endeavors to defend and decipher the mysteries concealed in the sea profundities, it becomes basic to recognize the interconnectedness of these drives with more extensive ecological and moral contemplations. The ecological difficulties, including the effect of environmental change on lowered locales, highlight the requirement for continuous coordinated effort among archeologists and natural researchers.

The moral obligations, enveloping issues of proprietorship, social responsiveness, and the protection of human remaining parts, feature the significance of comprehensive and dependable practices in sea prehistoric studies.

The cooperative and interdisciplinary nature of these continuous endeavors turns into a model for tending to the intricacies intrinsic in investigating the sea profundities. The difficulties presented by submerged conditions, combined with the basic to reveal and preserve sea legacy, request an amicable cooperation between different partners. Archeologists, researchers, policymakers, nearby networks, and the public structure an aggregate embroidery, each string adding to the more extensive story of oceanic paleontology.

Past the prompt victories and difficulties lies the ceaseless requirement for constant improvement and variation inside sea antiquarianism. The excursion to defend and decipher the mysteries concealed in the sea profundities requires a relentless obligation to getting the hang of, developing strategies, and coordinating different viewpoints. In this continuous story, the mission for information is a powerful power that pushes us into strange regions while requesting reflection and refinement in our methodologies.

The development of mechanical progressions stays a urgent part of the continuous endeavors in sea paleohistory. Coordinated efforts among archeologists and architects drive the advancement of state of the art instruments and methods that upgrade our ability to investigate and archive submerged locales. From cutting edge imaging frameworks to modern remotely worked vehicles, these developments work with more effective investigation as well as add to the accuracy and precision of information assortment.

The incorporation of Man-made brainpower (simulated intelligence) and AI into submerged investigation addresses an outskirts that holds monstrous commitment. Cooperative undertakings among archeologists and technologists are saddling the abilities of man-made intelligence to dissect huge datasets, recognize designs, and smooth out the handling of data. This cooperative methodology speeds up the speed of revelation as well as permits archeologists to zero in on the nuanced understanding of discoveries, enhancing the profundity of information got from lowered locales.

The continuous drives likewise spotlight the basic of cultivating worldwide coordinated effort in oceanic paleohistory. The sea, with its tremendous spans and interconnected biological systems, rises above international limits. Cooperative endeavors between countries, establishments, and analysts become vital for address worldwide difficulties, share ability, and guarantee the aggregate security of submerged social legacy.

The UNESCO Show on the Security of the Submerged Social Legacy remains as a foundation in advancing worldwide cooperation. This structure urges nations to team up in shielding lowered destinations and lays out standards for dependable investigation and conservation.

The cooperation encouraged by such peaceful accords guarantees that the mysteries concealed in the sea profundities are treated with the regard they merit on a worldwide scale.

Besides, the continuous endeavors accentuate the significance of interdisciplinary cooperation. The marriage of archeological skill with bits of knowledge from natural science, innovation, protection, and social investigations shapes an all encompassing way to deal with understanding and safeguarding lowered social legacy. Cooperative undertakings that unite assorted ranges of abilities and points of view enhance the investigation interaction as well as add to the improvement of complete techniques for protection and translation.

The eventual fate of sea archaic exploration lies in revealing secret fortunes as well as in tending to squeezing natural worries. Environmental change, contamination, and other anthropogenic variables present dangers to the very destinations that archeologists try to investigate and secure. Cooperative drives among archeologists and ecological researchers are imperative in creating versatile methodologies to moderate the effect of these dangers and guarantee the drawn out manageability of submerged social legacy.

Public commitment stays a key part in the continuous endeavors to shield and decipher oceanic secrets. Cooperative ventures that focus on openness, inclusivity, and training empower a more extensive crowd to interface with the miracles of the sea profundities. The narrating part of sea paleohistory, enhanced through cooperative endeavors with producers, instructors, and legacy translators, changes lowered antiques into accounts that resound with individuals from different foundations.

The continuous coordinated effort among archeologists and the media fills in as an extension that traverses the hole between scholastic examination and public comprehension. Narratives, presentations, and instructive projects not just bring the tales of submerged social legacy to life yet additionally rouse a feeling of marvel and interest in our sea past. Cooperative narrating turns into an amazing asset in democratizing information, guaranteeing that the fortunes concealed in the sea profundities are not bound to scholarly circles however are open to a worldwide crowd.

As we ponder the continuous endeavors to defend and decipher the mysteries concealed in the sea profundities, the account reaches out past the actual curios. It incorporates an aggregate excursion of investigation, cooperation, and variation — an excursion that looks for not exclusively to unwind secrets yet to encourage a significant comprehension of our common human legacy. The difficulties experienced along this excursion act as impetuses for development, welcoming archeologists, researchers, networks, and general society to meet up in a cooperative soul that rises above limits and guarantees the getting through tradition of sea paleontology for a long time into the future.